WHAT YOUR CHILDHOOD MEMORIES SAY ABOUT YOU

(AND WHAT YOU CAN DO ABOUT IT)

WHAT YOUR
CHILDHOOD
SAY

DR. KEVIN LEMAN

MEMORIES
ABOUT
YOU

{ *And What You Can Do About It* }

TYNDALE HOUSE PUBLISHERS, INC.
CAROL STREAM, ILLINOIS

Visit Tyndale's exciting Web site at www.tyndale.com

TYNDALE and Tyndale's quill logo are registered trademarks of Tyndale House Publishers, Inc.

What Your Childhood Memories Say about You . . . And What You Can Do about It

Designed by Erik Peterson

Edited by Dave Greene and Ramona Cramer Tucker

Library of Congress Cataloging-in-Publication Data

Leman, Kevin.
  What your childhood memories say about you-- and what you can do about it / Kevin Leman.
    p. cm.
  Includes bibliographical references.
  ISBN-13: 978-1-4143-1186-9 (hc)
  ISBN-10: 1-4143-1186-9 (hc)
  ISBN-13: 978-1-4143-1187-6 (sc)
  ISBN-10: 1-4143-1187-7 (sc)
  1. Early memories. 2. Self-perception. 3. Psychoanalysis. I. Title.
  BF378.E17L46 2007
  153.1′3—dc22   2007002213

Printed in the United States of America

13 12 11 10
 7   6   5

Dedication

Affectionately dedicated to
my sister, Sally Leman Chall,
who endured such things as me waking her up
by dangling a juicy night crawler in front of her nose,
and to my brother, Dr. John (Jack) E. Leman Jr.,
whom I referred to as "God" when I was in junior high
because he acted like God.

Do you remember the time we took a bus to the plaza
(the archaic name for a mall)
and went to the five-and-dime W. T. Grant Store,
which had a luncheonette in the back?
When I looked at the menu, I really wanted a turkey sandwich,
but that cost an exorbitant 80 cents,
when hamburgers were only 20 cents and cheeseburgers, 25 cents.
I'll never forget your response, Sally: "Kevin, get what you want."
And you meant it.
I couldn't help thinking, *She must really love me.*
That's how you make me feel, even today, decades later.

Jack, you pounded me many a day, but you also stuck up for me.
I'll always remember you allowing me to wear
your #12 football jersey to school.
That meant a great deal then—and it still does now.
Not to mention the 1965 Mustang convertible you gave me.

You two are still my heroes,
and I love you.
Thanks for putting up with your lastborn brother's antics
through all the great growing-up years
in western New York state.

Contents

Acknowledgments

A special thanks to Dave Greene for his research, editing, and great contributions behind the scenes . . .

Think Back . . . Way Back

What's locked away in your mind?

What are your earliest childhood memories?

In all my years of private practice and in conversations following weekend seminars, I've asked people tens of thousands of questions about themselves, their relationships, and their families. I've probed parents about their greatest challenges in raising their kids, addressed corporate bigwigs about the psychology of doing business, and heard enough about married couples' sex lives to turn anyone's face seven shades of red. But of all the questions I've asked in those interactions, no single question gets minds working across the board like the one about early childhood memories.

You see, the answers I receive from six-year-olds to seasoned CEOs earning six figures reveal more about the people answering than any other question. "Why is that?" you ask. Because those answers provide a priceless glimpse past all the facades and defenses, straight into the core of who a person is. They are a master key that unlocks all sorts of entries into what makes a person tick. All the money in the world can't buy what you can learn from your early childhood memories, just like spending years trying to figure yourself out can never uncover what you can learn by exploring those memories.

Maybe you picked up this book because you're intrigued by what life-changing insights your seemingly mundane childhood memories might reveal about who you are. Perhaps you already have a few memories in mind, and you're wondering what they might have to say about you. If that describes you, read on, for this book is about precisely that—how your childhood memories reveal who you really are.

Or you may be thinking, *But Dr. Leman, childhood was such a long time ago. What can my random memories possibly have to say that would be of any value now that I'm a grown-up? Why dwell on the past when there's nothing I can do to change it?*

But what if your childhood memories aren't random? What if they are there for a reason? And what if understanding who you are, revealed through those memories, has everything to do with how you live in the present and how successfully you are able to take control of your future?

If you don't listen to who you are, you may always find yourself reliving a history you'd rather not repeat. While you can't change your past, you can change the way you understand it and move forward in light of that understanding. Do that, and it will make all the difference in not only your life, but in the lives of those around you—your friends, relatives, acquaintances, and colleagues.

> While you can't *change* your past, you can change the way you *understand* it and move forward in light of that understanding.

I'd also like to say a word to all you guys who picked up this book or had it handed to you. In my experience, we men are much more hesitant, by nature, to embrace "all this memory stuff" and the process of "digging into our feelings." So if you're a guy, it's likely you'll want to change channels on me before hearing me out. But while you're channel surfing through the beginning of this book, consider two things:

1. If you want tools to help you get where you'd like to go in your marriage or dating relationship, in the parenting of your kids, in your career, or in life in general, hear me out for one chapter. By

then, if you can't see anything that might apply to you, use the book for kindling on a cold winter evening.

2. Even if you're hesitant to delve into your own childhood memories, I challenge you to learn to use these tools as you listen to the memories and feelings of your loved ones. They'll thank you for it . . . whether now or down the road.

What if, through one simple question, you could get inside the head of someone you're close to and find out exactly what makes them tick? how they see themselves and the world around them? I'm not exaggerating when I say that you could avoid years, if not decades, of misunderstanding by considering the themes of your loved ones' childhood memories.

You may have terrible memories from your childhood . . . horrific memories that no one should ever have to live through. Especially a child. If this has been your experience, and you've placed those memories in a vault, locked them away, and buried the key, who could blame you? But, by doing so, what else—besides your memories—have you placed in that vault?

May I gently suggest that perhaps you've climbed in there yourself, closed the door, and locked it behind you? If so, you may be effectively locking out those who could help you. If this book can, in any way, begin to free you from the hold those memories have on you, there's nothing I'd rather accomplish.

Whether you are curious, skeptical, excited, bruised, or in pain, your childhood memories hold the key to understanding who you are right now so you might find freedom and fulfillment.

After decades as a psychologist, I've seen enough evidence to offer you as close to a Midas-muffler guarantee as possible: Tell me three of your early childhood memories, and I'll tell you what weighs you down and what motivates you forward, what causes you to lose sleep at night with worry and what keeps you up with excitement—in short, what makes you you.

It's a tall order, I know. But consider just a handful of examples as we start:

- Civil rights activist Martin Luther King Jr. remembers his father walking confidently out of a shoe store in segregated downtown Atlanta when the clerk said the two had to move to the back of the store before being helped.[1]

- Real-estate mogul Donald Trump, who now owns large portions of Manhattan but loves the thrill of the deal as much as making money, remembers gluing together his brother's building blocks because he was so pleased with the building he had made.[2]

- Mother Teresa, one of the most well-respected saints our generation has seen as she reached out to the poor and dying in Calcutta, recalls her family gathering together each evening to pray and her mother bringing the poor and hungry into their house for meals.[3]

- Computer whiz and entrepreneur Bill Gates, now the richest man in the world, remembers negotiating a written contract with his sister for five dollars, giving him unlimited access to her baseball mitt.[4]

- Evangelist Billy Graham, who has introduced millions to a relationship with God, recalls his own father calling to him from across a grassy field, saying, "Billy Frank, come to Daddy. C'mon to Daddy."[5]

Out of the hundreds of thousands of possible memories that those individuals could have had growing up, why did *those* particular memories stick out and stay with them for decades? Could it be that during their early childhood years, which psychologists agree form the most critical years of our development, the pieces of who they would be for the rest of their lives were already coming together and beginning to create a picture, revealed in those memories?

I firmly believe so and maintain that the childhood experiences you remember—and the particular way in which you remember them—reveal who you are. By identifying and understanding those memories, you can gather invaluable information.

What if your memories *could* decode the mysteries of who you are?

Do you sometimes wonder *why* you do the things you do? why you find yourself repeating certain mistakes or bumping up against the same obstacles time after time? What if your memories could decode the mysteries of who you are? What if you were able to understand why you think, feel, and respond the way you do—and to use those revelations to take steps toward positive changes you'd like to make for your future? Changes that would help you become who you really are, instead of who you may be trying to be? Think of the stress that would take out of your life!

Let's face it. It's taken years for you to learn to be the person you are, so you're not going to change overnight. But the good news is that you can unlearn those aspects that you want to change and chart a new path in life. And it's never too late to start, whether you're 20, 40, 60, or 80!

Early childhood memories are simply a tool to help you understand what makes you tick. They don't have anything to do with slipping into a googly eyed trance because of some hypnotist's swinging pocket watch. Exploring your memories simply involves looking at the pieces that you've stored in your mind and asking, *Why do I remember those particular events? Why not others? Do those memories reveal anything about who I am?*

Ask yourself, *Why do I remember those particular events? Why not others? Do those memories reveal anything about who I am?*

You may be surprised how much of a treasure trove your

childhood memories really are. You may discover things about yourself that you might never have discovered otherwise: how you perceive yourself and the world around you, your fears and aspirations, even your strengths and weaknesses. In fact, your childhood memories also hold keys to

- how you relate to others;
- your interests (including hobbies and possible careers);
- whether you're more comfortable working with people or things; and
- how you deal with emotions.

So think back—way back—to your childhood. (Okay, for most of you it's probably not as far back as *I* have to go.) I'll ask that million-dollar question again: What are *your* earliest childhood memories?

Have you got one? Do you find more surfacing as you begin thinking back to your family, your childhood friends, and the schools you attended? Even if you're thinking, *Dr. Leman, I can't remember where I left my keys five minutes ago let alone what I was thinking or feeling decades ago,* stay with me and I'll help jog your memory in the chapters to come.

Together we'll look at why you remember what you remember. We'll explore some of the common themes that emerge and how those themes reveal the kind of person you are. And because many of us also have painful memories, I'll reveal how you can "change" them through confronting the lies you tell yourself about them. Finally, we'll look at how your discoveries about your early childhood memories can help in your relationships and in your work. We're in for quite a journey!

But first, let me show you how all this works by telling you some of my early childhood memories.

I Made a Fool of Myself . . . and Liked It!

Why your private logic shows in public

Once when I was eight, my older sister, Sally, got the idea to dress me up in my billy-goat sweatshirt as the mascot for her varsity cheerleading squad. My task was easy. I was supposed to run onto the court with the cheerleaders in front of the crowded hometown gymnasium bleachers during a time-out to perform the five-second Williamsville Billies cheer, complete with hand motions. Decades later I still remember that cheer: "Basket, basket, score, score, score. Williamsville Central, we want more!"

Five seconds and a few hand motions—it wasn't exactly Shakespearean acting. Any joker could have pulled it off.

But somehow I managed to mess it up. It was the most itty-bitty part you could ever have, and I got the hand motions wrong. When I realized what I'd done, I froze. Row upon row of kids and adults began laughing at me, turning to their friends and pointing, then elbowing other friends to get a look at the fool up front. In that instant I felt the sharp sting of embarrassment.

But what happened next defines the memory for me . . . and perhaps for reasons other than what you might expect. The most memorable part of those seconds on the gym floor was not the initial embarrassment. It was the much stronger—and surprising—feeling that followed. The entire school body was pointing at me and laughing, but as I looked around I thought to myself, *Hey, this really isn't so bad.*

Believe it or not, I didn't care that others thought I'd made a fool of myself. What was so much more important to me was that I had made people laugh. And not only was playing the part of the joker not so bad, it was great. I loved it! I felt so good giving all those students a laugh at my expense that I probably would have taken my botched Williamsville Billies cheer to the *Ed Sullivan Show* on TV, if they'd invited me.

In that moment, burned so vividly into my memory that I can still clearly recall it over half a century later, I identified a vital part of who I'd always been and who I would always be: Kevin Leman the Joker. Far from being an ace student like my sister or a star athlete like my brother, I was different all right, having seemingly emerged straight out of the little clown car in our family's three-ring circus.

It wasn't long after that botched cheer on the basketball court that someone egged me on at another home game to attack Williamsville's rival mascot—the Amherst Tiger of Amherst Central High School. I ran up behind the dumb cat, ripped its tail completely off, and went prancing around our gym twirling that tail above my head, whipping the home crowd into a frenzy. I was having the time of my life! Shortly after that game, our school newspaper ran a good-size headline that read, "Demon Leman Defeats Amherst Tiger in Half-Time Bout."

> I was different all right, having seemingly emerged straight out of the little clown car in our family's three-ring circus.

That was me: Leman the Demon. I had found my calling. I was making a fool of myself . . . and loving it!

Is What's Private Showing in Public?

You may read that memory of mine and be completely unable to relate to it. In fact, you may even have a similar childhood memory of thoroughly embarrassing yourself in public—yet the way you reacted to your circumstances was completely different from how I reacted to mine. You may remember that same sting of embarrassment upon realizing that you'd messed up a line in the school play, a violin solo at your recital, or a pirouette during a ballet performance. But instead of feeling the euphoria of having people chuckle at you, you were horrified. If that's one of your childhood memories, you may never want to step in front of another crowd again. Comedian Jerry Seinfeld jokes that people are generally so scared of public speaking that they would rather be lying in the coffin at a funeral than in front of the crowd delivering the eulogy![1]

I once read that Michael Jordan said he was never as comfortable as when he was on the basketball court. I can't fly through the air like Jordan (although I do have a three-inch vertical leap), but I can relate to his feeling of stepping into a well-defined comfort zone. I'm completely in my element the instant the blinding stage lights go on, the floor director of a TV show points at me, and I "go live." In fact, I once stumbled into our kitchen in the early morning hours, opened the refrigerator door, and when the light inside went on, I launched into a monologue before realizing I was there for a glass of milk!

Today, when I stand in front of a crowd of five thousand adults or prepare to walk onto the set of a TV show before a viewing audience of millions, I get a twinkle in my eye and think, *Hey, this looks like fun.* As amazing as it might seem, I can't wait to get up in front—and the larger the crowd the better. You, however, might look at that same crowd and feel a wave of nausea, break out in a cold sweat, and think, *Before I get in front of those people, I'll hang myself with my own shoelaces! There is no way I'm going to do that . . . ever!* One of my greatest pleasures may very well be your worst nightmare. And vice versa.

But when you think about it, that shouldn't surprise you, because when two people are in a similar situation, there are a zillion and one ways they will not see the world precisely the same. That unique perspective is called "private logic," a term coined by psychologist Alfred Adler. Your private logic encompasses the way you see yourself and your view of life; it includes the way you seek attention or handle conflict. It's revealed through how you complete the phrase "And the moral of my life's story is . . ."

> Your private logic is revealed through how you complete the phrase "And the moral of my life's story is . . ."

It suggests how you are inclined to respond when a waiter spills a drink down the front of your shirt or when you suddenly come upon the rear bumper of an elderly person driving a blistering 43 mph on the freeway. Do you respond by acknowledging that accidents happen and that elderly people are to be shown grace? Or do you see those incidents as direct affronts against you or maddening obstacles that cause you to push back? or, even further, as events in a world conspiring against you?

In short, your private logic is your subjective interpretation of the people, places, and things around you—a perspective that changes over time but that's built upon the solid, immovable foundation of your formative, early childhood years.

As the youngest child in my family, I accepted early on that my role was to entertain people, to have fun, and to push limits whenever possible. The only way I could stand out from my scholarly sister and athletic brother was to cut my own path, which was by being a goof-off. Some children strive for attention in positive ways; others strive for attention in negative ways. But one way or another, all kids strive for attention. And getting a laugh at all costs—even if it meant getting to know the principal a bit better—was how I "logically" understood my role in life.

If you grew up living to make people laugh, as I did, then you'll see yourself as a clown with the world as your three-ring circus. If you grew up as a martyr, believing that everyone in the world is part of some secret underground society sworn to overthrow your success, then you'll continue to view life that way. Your private logic is shaped both by who you innately were when you were born and who you became through your family environment. Even children within the same family—as much as they may adopt similar values, speak a common body language, and understand the same inside jokes—will view the same moment in childhood differently. One might remember Dad's admonitions not to play near the street as overbearing and distrustful. Another might remember Dad's watchful eye as lovingly protective.

5

The way you respond to each and every moment in your life reveals how you see yourself and the world. And as you examine your collection of childhood memories, you'll begin to discover themes—themes that reveal your own private logic as clearly as the grain in a piece of wood.

Going against the Grain

Did you ever take a woodshop class in school or sit around at summer camp whittling a stick? If you did, you know that if you ever try to carve against the grain, all you'll get is a pile of chips and a handful of splinters. You'll have much better luck if you carve along the grain. Then you can create different shapes, sand it to soften its feel, stain it to change its color, varnish it to protect it, and polish it to make it shine. But guess what? No matter what, the grain of the wood remains the same.

That wood grain is a lot like your personality. Whatever your strengths and weaknesses, you can sand what you've been given to soften your rough edges, add stain and polish to make a beautiful first impression, and varnish it to protect yourself from corrupting influences. But living a life that goes completely against your natural personality will ultimately give you "splinters."

> Living a life that goes completely against your natural personality will ultimately give you splinters.

Here's a great example. I should never become an accountant, for the only figure I'm interested in is my wife, Sande's. If I had to spend an hour, let alone my entire working life, with a spreadsheet, I'd give up and join the circus, where my chances for success would be much greater. Numbers are great things, I admit. They help me identify my favorite college basketball and football players during game time and are very useful in assessing how much weight I'm gaining by my pants size. But beyond that, I have little use for them. It's simply not in me to spend hours crunching numbers. By knowing myself, I avoid the splinters of going against my grain.

It's not enough to simply know my grain, though, because we can "go with our grain" in both positive and negative ways. I can go with my grain in positive ways by helping people laugh—I love doing that when I speak, write, or run into some of you in the grocery store line. In some ways I really do see the world as one big stand-up comedy stage. But I can go with my grain in negative ways as Leman the Mischievous Demon, first cousin to Dennis the Menace, getting into all sorts of trouble and occasionally looking at the line drawn in front of me and stepping over it just for fun.

Let me show you what I mean by telling you two stories from my life.

My wife, Sande, loves antiques. This past Christmas she bought some antique ornaments that are beautiful but costly! After I'd gotten over my sticker shock, I couldn't help but chuckle because where Sande saw them as works of art, I remembered target practice. You see, those antique Christmas ornaments took me back to when I was a kid, perched on the living-room steps like a sniper with my BB pistol. It wasn't exactly a high-powered firearm. In fact, the BB's trajectory even had a bit of a lob to it. But I saw myself as the Delta Force point man on *Operation Tinsel* and made it my mission to pick off as many Christmas tree ornaments as I could. And because I did it from across the room, no one could see me, so they blamed it on the family cat. Who knows how many dollars' worth of ornaments I picked off as a child . . . ornaments that would have survived to become antiques but for my sharpshooting practice!

It sounds terrible, I know—just the sort of thing Dennis the Menace and I might dream up in a brainstorming session—but when I chose to follow my fun-loving grain in mischievous, rebellious ways, I sometimes stepped across that line of what is appropriate. And that propensity to play the rebel has surfaced again and again throughout my life.

For example, when I was working as a janitor in the Tucson Medical Center, I met the love of my life, Sande, who was a nurse's aide at the time. I was completely smitten with Sande's beauty, grace, and class, but her boss there told her not to associate with me because "I wouldn't amount to much."

Years later, after I'd advanced at that same university to become an assistant dean of students and gotten the woman of my dreams to marry me in spite of her boss's advice, I was helping with registration one day. I spotted that very same woman, Sande's former boss, standing in line. Out of the thousands who were there on campus registering that day, she had coincidentally appeared in my line to sign up for some ongoing education. I couldn't believe how the tables had turned! Thankfully there were seven people before her in line so I could consider my response to her. As the minutes ticked by, I could feel the little angel and demon on my shoulders locking halo and horns, wrestling it out as to whether I'd be gracious to her or get even!

When she stepped to the front of the line, she clearly didn't recognize who I was. She told me what classes she was registering for, and I looked thoughtfully over her registration cards.

"Sorry," I said as I frowned and shook my head. "You'll need to go to the TBA building to get signatures on these cards. It's located at the very far end of campus." As I handed her back her cards, she thanked me and headed off on her long trek in search of the TBA building . . . which didn't exist. I had simply glanced at one of the papers on my table and seen the letters T-B-A—To Be Announced—beside one of the classes and had made the whole scenario up on the spot!

I know, I know. It wasn't a very kind joke. Like all of us, I have my weaknesses. Part of my grain—my propensity to certain ways of thinking or acting, if you will—is to take my fun-loving grain and put a mischievous twist on it. I do this much less today, however (except for tapping on the brake from time to time when someone is tailgating me), for as I matured I came to find that being a rebellious joker began to work to my detriment.

After my run-in with the Amherst Tiger mascot, I took to my role as Leman the Demon with reckless abandon. I threw water balloons in class. I crawled out of a classroom on my hands and knees while the teacher was teaching just to get a laugh from my peers. I carried a dictionary through the hallways with the pages cut out to conceal a water gun that I could whip out, squirt a teacher, then hide. I even set fire to the wastebasket in English class. That was my idea of fun!

But fun only got me so far.

You see, getting people to laugh was an important part of who I was and still am. Kevin Leman was both innately wired and nurtured growing up to be a comedian. But I was also telling myself a lie back then: that I didn't matter in life unless I was making others laugh. With all the brilliance of a frog refusing to jump from a pot of slowly boiling water, I maintained my trickster persona with my crazy antics—and slowly it was killing me.

Finally my high school geometry teacher, Ms. Eleanor Wilson, pulled me aside. "Kevin, I've watched your behavior. I've seen the way you act at school and how you relate to your peers. And do you know what I think? You could really make something of your life if you used the skills you have. I see your potential, but applying yourself is up to you. I can't make that happen."

I was stunned. She was the first person—other than my parents, and parents are supposed to say things like that—who had dared to speak the truth. That interaction with Ms. Wilson literally changed the direction of my life.

Are You Being Deceived?

I've told that story about Ms. Wilson many times before, but I mention it briefly again here because it touches on one of the most important points of this book, which we'll examine in more detail in later chapters: There are all sorts of lies you tell yourself over and over until you accept them as readily as you do your own skin. And it isn't always easy to recognize them as lies. Sometimes it takes a Ms. Wilson, a friend, or a book like this one to reveal the truth.

> There are all sorts of lies you tell yourself over and over until you accept them as readily as you do your own skin.

That's where your childhood memories come in, pointing to what makes you you and providing clues to your strengths and weaknesses. What my memory of botching the hand motions to that cheer and making the student body laugh tells me is that I love the spotlight.

I enjoy being in front of people so much, in fact, that I've made a living of it, while helping others learn a thing or two about themselves and their relationships in the process. If I ever forget that lesson and sign up for a career in accounting, I'll quickly degenerate into a miserable jellyfish of a human being. But there's also a flip side to my love of the spotlight: Too much attention may not be a good thing for me. If I hadn't confronted the lie in my life years ago that said I only mattered if I was making headlines in people's days, I might have continued to revert to that negative-attention-getting clown that my early childhood memories reveal I can be.

And that's another lesson that has literally changed my life.

We all walk around with lies. You might relate to the lesson I learned from my memory—that drawing too much attention to yourself may not be a good thing—in a different way. You might tend to draw inappropriate attention to yourself by the way you act, the way you dress, or by the car you drive. The lesson for you, then, could be that to have a healthy mental state in the present and in the future, it's more important that you notice others instead of seeking to have them notice you.

You see, lies drive a wedge between who you really are and who you act like you are, and the greater the distance between those two, the greater the dissonance in your life will be. Let's say you tell yourself that you're in shape because you once played college volleyball and ran a mile and a half every other day 11 years ago. Or that even though you haven't exercised since before the Berlin Wall fell, you still see yourself as athletic. Why do you think so many middle-aged men hurt themselves playing pickup games of football? Could it be that, in spite of the fact that their bodies have gained well-padded front and rear bumpers, they still live as legends in their own minds? They haven't yet learned to see themselves as they really are. But as you recognize the truth and work toward embracing it, the gap between the ideal and the real closes—and the closer the distance between these two, the better.

Many of us look at the grain of our wood and decide that it's good only for throwing into a wood chipper or mashing into pulp. But that's not at all how Almighty God sees you. He can work all things together for good, we're told.[2] All things! Even your flaws, your imperfections, the grain that seems unworkable—somehow he takes even those aspects and works them into his ongoing creative masterpiece. The Renaissance artist Michelangelo carved his famous statue *David* from a block of marble that had been already rejected by two other sculptors because of an imperfection.[3] You may be all too conscious of your own blemishes and feel like that imperfect, rejected block (or an imperfect blockhead), but the Master Artist, who knows what you're made of better than you do, takes your worst flaws and incorporates them into the beauty of his creation—you!

Truth is, you're one of a kind. And that's a very good thing.

One-of-a-Kind Memories

You've probably heard that age-old quip of the psychologist saying to a client, "Tell me about your mother." The reason we shrinks ask that question and others like it is because asking about dear old Mom helps reveal patterns, and psychology is a science of recognizing patterns in human behavior.

If you and I were to sit next to each other on an airplane and we began making small talk for a few minutes as the crew revved up the engines, by the time we were taxiing down the runway I could tell you some things about the way you see yourself, your family, and the world around you. If I were to ask you a few probing questions as we rocketed through the clouds, I could tell you even more about yourself. Why? Because I've spent decades exploring patterns in human behavior.

You can learn an awful lot from family environments, parenting styles you were exposed to as you grew up, and your birth order. Your unique, innate, God-given traits and your family environment both contribute to who you are. Your birth order and your personality type contribute to who you are. The circumstances you faced as a family in your childhood years and the way people have related to you over the decades contribute to who you are. All of these provide entry points to describing patterns of human behavior, but what they can't describe are certain other aspects, such as whether you're more apt to be a homebody or an adventurous world traveler, or whether speed thrills or terrifies you.

What makes exploring your childhood memories so wonderful

is that memories target who you are specifically because you yourself stored them. They give you unique insights into the tough challenges of your life, into what you do well, into your comfort zone, and into your fears. They reveal your strengths and weaknesses, what you like to do, and what you don't like to do.

Take this memory of mine, which provides unique insight into my personal interests. I was five years old, lying on my bed, bored in that midsummer way that only kids can be, with the last day of school a distant memory and back-to-school sales a long way off. Then I heard a buzz. I was so bored it could have been coming from inside my head—static on the brain! But as I lay there on the bed listening, I realized that it was a single-engine airplane buzzing slowly across the sky over our house. And as I listened, something within me was ignited and burned into my consciousness.

There's no way that John and May Leman's parenting style or my birth order could have predicted that I would love to travel, since we as a family didn't travel much at all when I was growing up. But today it's a truism that Kevin Leman is a traveling man. These days airplanes seem to serve as my home away from home. I've flown nearly four million miles on American Airlines—that's eight round-trips to the moon! Not that I'd move into a 747 and set up the family photos on the armrests, mind you, for the sake of living in a metal tube with claustrophobic bathrooms. It's what airline travel opens up to me that I love: flying around the country, meeting wonderful people in new places, and talking with them about their families. I love encouraging them that they can make it in life, that there is something they have to offer the world that no one else does.

I believe that memory stuck in my mind because I wanted to travel even as a young child. As I lay there on that bed, I remember feeling a desire to explore other places, to see what lay beyond our own little town.

In a world where we compare everyone to everyone else, the bot-

There is no other you. There never was. There never will be.

tom line is that you're one of a kind. There is no other you. There never was. There never will be. Even identical twins have different fingerprints. God broke the mold when he made you. And hidden within your childhood memories are the secrets to your unique traits—traits you may not even know you have.

You now hold the key. All you have to do is use it to open the door.

A thrilling, life-changing journey awaits!

CHAPTER 2

The Little Boy or Girl You Once Were, You Still Are

The consistency factor rides again

Once when I was a kid, I toddled out of our home onto the front porch. It was early on a Sunday morning, before anyone else in my family was awake. Why I did this I have no idea. Three-year-olds aren't noted for their logic. Perhaps the paperboy had just dropped off the morning edition and I went out to investigate the noise. Perhaps I simply stepped out to see what was happening in our suburban Buffalo, New York, neighborhood of Kenmore. But there I was, staring at the thick Sunday newspaper lying by my feet and the three concrete steps that dropped to our sidewalk when I heard the door click behind me.

I turned around to get back in, but the door was locked. If that wasn't bad enough for a little tot, I began to feel my bowels crying out for a potty! I pounded on the door as hard as a three-year-old could and yelled for my family, but no one heard me. I remember feeling helpless, panicky, and a little irritated that no one heard me pounding on the door. *How could they not hear me?!* I remember thinking. Nature wasn't just calling; it was screaming! Finally, when I couldn't wait any longer, I messed my pants . . . right there on the front porch.

Among the hundreds of thousands of moments that I could have possibly remembered growing up, why in the world does that memory stick out among all the others? I know for a fact that I had plenty of happy experiences unwrapping presents on Christmas mornings, riding my bike outside on humid summer days, and eating cake at birthday parties. But in spite of all the pleasant moments I experienced as a child, what sticks out in my mind is messing my pants on the front porch and yelling for someone—anyone—to let me in!

And since then, I've spent my whole life banging on doors! Consider the following:

- I banged on countless doors throughout my school years with crazy antics so my peers and teachers would notice me.
- I literally banged on door after door selling magazines.
- I banged on 160 college doors with my college applications before North Park College finally broke down and let me in. Even the night school at the State University of New York at Buffalo turned me down. *Night school!*
- I banged on the door of *The Phil Donahue Show* 14 times (I have the rejection letters to prove it) before they finally let me appear on it.

In fact, throughout my life I've felt that I've often been on the outside looking in, or being held back by others, waiting to be turned loose.

Yes, that little gem is my earliest childhood memory—and I believe it's there for a reason. I have had a difficult time "getting my foot in the door" in life and have always felt that I'm trying to make my voice heard. And that memory of being locked out of the house is consistent with how I view life.

Here's what I mean. When I was a kid, I was very physically active, so my mother—even with eyes in the back of her head—often lost me when I ran out of the house into the neighborhood. I was a toddling little escapee (that's probably why I was out on our front porch that Sunday morning in the first place!). This led to another of my earliest childhood memories, which was literally being put on a harness leash attached to a dog run between an elm and a maple tree to keep me out of trouble. I asked my mother decades later, "Did you think I had Irish setter blood in me or something?" Years later, in another incident that fed my feeling of being thwarted by others, the school district super-intendent pulled my girlfriend's father aside and told him not to let his daughter associate with me because I was never going to amount to anything—a line I would hear again and again throughout my life.

Consequently, I developed an I'll-show-you attitude to fight the leashes and locked doors, and that attitude became a life theme for me. It was a pattern that started way back in my childhood and continued well into adulthood.

The Consistency Factor

Naturally, the way you see life changes over time. Thankfully, my days of pounding on doors at television studios and radio stations are over. Now people warmly open them to the chubby little psychologist from Tucson. Still, from time to time, I feel that same fight-or-flight response just beneath the surface when I believe that the world is closing its doors on me, because that experience is so engrained in my past.

No matter how you see the world today and no matter how much you've changed, you always carry inside of you at least the residue of that child's perspective you once had, if not a strong propensity to fall back into those early patterns. When you develop a way of understanding the world and your place in it during those early, formative years as a child, that private logic serves as your compass for the decisions you make, the words that come from your mouth, and the actions that follow. You don't change your inner motivation from day to day, switching randomly for no reason. Instead, we all follow our own well-worn paths, a tendency I call the "consistency factor," which says that the way you see the world today is consistent with the way you learned the world operated as a child.

> The way you see the world *today* is consistent with the way you learned the world operated as a child.

Let me illustrate. A woman told me about one of her early childhood memories, which involved sitting next to a boy in the backseat of a car while her father was driving. As they turned sharply around a corner, the inertia caused the boy to tumble toward her, and he ended up on top of her. The strongest part of the woman's memory was sitting up and seeing the disapproving look of her father from the front seat.

As a little girl, she was already experiencing her father's critical eye toward her interaction with the opposite sex. There was a cold distance between herself and the one male in the entire world that she should have had the closest relationship with back then—her own father. No wonder that, later in life, that woman had trouble with intimacy with guys. She obviously perceived her father as a stern authoritarian, and even as a young girl felt very uncomfortable about being close to the opposite sex. As an adult, that woman was still holding people at arm's length, rarely initiating conversation, and fearful of physical contact—a situation you could have anticipated decades before from her childhood memories.

That isn't to say that our childhood memories define us forever, because that certainly needn't be the case. But we're all familiar with our tendency to fall into a rut, reverting to those old, well-worn patterns. Perhaps you've struggled with habitually trying to please others, responding to everyone's needs but your own. Sure, you're good at coming through when people need you—even developing a reputation for helping others pull through in a crisis—but you do it whatever the cost. But let's say that as part of your personal growth, you began feeling the effects of operating as a pleaser in your own relationships and commitments and recognized that you had to give something up before you gave out. And so you began making changes, saying no to requests and allowing yourself to do what you needed to survive instead of always thinking of others first.

Sounds like you've overcome that old private logic, doesn't it?

But then what if a neighbor comes to you with "a desperate need" to have you watch her two kids "for only a couple hours"? You know for a fact that you don't have the time to help, as you're supposed to finish a term paper that evening for your night-school class. You also know that there are others whom this person could probably call. Yet you begin wondering if you can write your paper while also keeping an eye on the kids in the other room.

Doesn't that scenario bring back your old private logic in a hurry?

Or try this scenario. You came from a very expressive family—sometimes perhaps too expressive—so you're aware that you occasionally step over the line in what you say, even though it is what you feel. But after hurting the feelings of friends, fellow church members, and family, you rightly realized that you needed to hold your tongue a bit more. You began watching what you said and thinking before you spoke. But then came an incident that really boiled your blood, a comment made that you believed was simply untrue.

In both cases, what do you feel inside? Even though you've been making healthy steps in the right direction, isn't it true that in each of these circumstances, you feel those deep, gut-level emotions kick in, and those tried-but-not-necessarily-so-true responses surface in you all over again? The private logic that you developed as a child isn't far behind you when push comes to shove, is it?

Even when you're able to make significant changes to your behavior over time, isn't it true that the little boy or girl you once were isn't far behind you?

Crucial Reference Points

As I neared the end of my senior year in high school, the fact that I was actually going to graduate hit me like a shock wave. *What have I been doing all this time?* I asked myself. While other kids around me were getting ready to shoot for the stars in college and their careers, I felt I was about to sail off the edge of my known world into oblivion. For me, school had always been about entertaining others, but now that my audience was moving on, not only was the show over, but a large part of my identity was crumbling.

I didn't know what to do with myself.

At various points throughout life, we arrive at a crossroads, where our self-understanding and our understanding of the world around us are thrown into scrutiny. I call these crossroads "crucial reference points." Reference points, because they are typically points in time that refer us back to our learned private logic; and crucial, because they usually involve significant life events with equally significant consequences.

> At various points throughout life, we arrive at a crossroads.

These crucial reference points often include separating from our parents, our first day at school, making new friends, the changes of puberty, growing feelings of attraction for the opposite sex, graduations, moving out of our parents' home, beginning a new career, marriage, having kids, etc. How many times have you heard someone say, "In high school I was a real goof-off, but in college I buckled down and got good grades"? That's an example of a crucial reference point (transition from high school to college) in which significant change was made ("I buckled down and got good grades") as the consequences of our old private logic were felt ("I was a real goof-off").

In every case, you'll find that these crucial reference points compel an inner response from your private logic, often tapping into those early, learned behaviors and testing the changes you've endeavored to make in your life over the years. These crucial reference points consistently show that your childhood responses are never far below the surface—even if your mature, adult response is 180 degrees different from what your childhood private logic is whispering to you.

Telling It Like It Is

Perhaps you've thought, *Why are we looking solely at childhood memories? Wouldn't it also help to look at more recent memories—the kind that keep me up at night now—or even those memories that stand out in my teenage years? Why childhood memories?*

> With children, what you see is what you get.

In short, the answer is because with children, what you see is what you get.

I talked with a couple whose young daughter had a rather embarrassing habit of playing with her genitals in public. Before it got any worse, they had to tell her that touching her vagina wasn't something she should do while she was in the grocery store produce section or at the local public library during story time.

One Sunday, following the evening church service, they invited their pastor over to their house. The parents were chatting with him when the conversation was interrupted by a voice from the next room.

"Mom-my," the girl called in a singsongy voice. "Guess where my fingers are?"

Children don't mince words. As refreshing or frightening as it may be, they're certainly honest—sometimes brutally honest. How often have you seen a child (perhaps your own) do such things as ask your sister during the family reunion photo, "Why are your teeth yellow?" Or say, "Mom, that woman is fat!" as you order burgers at the local fast-food joint. Surely you would never admit that's what you were thinking, even though you were thinking it. Children, however, wear their thoughts, opinions, and feelings on their sleeves. They speak what we adults have learned not to speak of.

Consequently, there isn't much gap between what's going on inside children and what's going on outside. Oh, sure, their imaginations run rampant, and they may spend half of their waking hours in make-believe land. But children's outer actions and inner memories reflect a foundational understanding of themselves and their environment. They are not convoluted by the mind games we adults play and masks we wear to present ourselves as someone other than who we really are.

Comedian Bill Cosby once remarked, "As I have discovered by examining my past, I started out as a child."[1] It's true. We all start out as children, and one thing psychologists agree on is that those early childhood years are the formative years in a person's life. All of us start from this place of straightforward, no-nonsense honesty, when our psyche told us like it was. If ever there were a time to capture a snapshot of who you are, childhood is that time. As we grow older, many of us get phonier and phonier with people, wearing mask upon mask to hide our flaws.

The answer to healthy adult behavior, however, is to find a way to embrace a new private logic—not to revert back to Neverland.

Are You Living in Neverland?

Few people would argue that Michael Jackson has proven to be one of the most popular musicians and entertainers of the twentieth century. His album *Thriller* remains one of the best-selling albums of all time. It probably comes as no surprise, then, that some of Michael's earliest childhood memories are about two of his main interests: singing and dancing.

"Every one of my albums or the group's albums has been dedicated to our mother, Katherine Jackson, since we took over our own careers and began to produce our own music," Michael said in his autobiography, *Moonwalk*. "My first memories are of her holding me and singing songs like 'You Are My Sunshine' and 'Cotton Fields.' She sang to me and to my brothers and sisters often."[2]

A memory like that seems in line for someone who became known as "the king of pop," doesn't it?

But there's a darker side to those cherished early memories, as he also admitted: "I remember singing at the top of my voice and dancing with real joy and working too hard for a child."[3]

"Working too hard for a child." Those sobering words provide a glimpse into the reality that Michael's stardom came with a price—that of his childhood.

Listen to another even-more-telling memory of his: "There was a park across the street from the Motown studio, and I can remember looking at those kids playing games. I'd just stare at them in wonder—I couldn't imagine such freedom, such a carefree life—and wish more than anything that I had that kind of freedom, that I could walk away and be like them."[4]

It's no wonder that the boy who lost so much of his childhood grew into a man trying to reclaim it. After he'd hit stardom, Michael bought over 2,800 acres in the San Rafael Mountains and established his Neverland Ranch.[5] There he built a zoo and an amusement park, complete with Ferris wheel, merry-go-round, and other rides.[6] As someone who lived so intently in the public eye even in his early childhood—who admitted that he wished "more than anything" that he could walk away from the recording studio to play—is it any surprise that Michael became as reclusive as he has? Is it any surprise that he created a place where he could escape and try in some way to reclaim his childhood?

Yet such a longing is still no excuse for his adult behavior. Michael's inability to cope with the pressures of stardom has wreaked havoc not only on his personal life but on others' lives as well.

The name for Jackson's Neverland Ranch, of course, comes from the classic children's story *Peter Pan*, about the boy who never wanted to grow up. In the story, Neverland is that place where kids stay kids, where play is the only real work, and where the pressures to grow up are always held at bay.

Sounds a lot like the way many of us adults live, doesn't it?

23

We all long to return to Neverland at times . . . that place where the little boy or girl we once were never grows up. In many ways, it's easier to jump on the merry-go-round of our own childhood private logic and ride it in circles, accepting the lies we tell ourselves that revert us back to our childlike behavior.

We all long to return to Neverland.

But if it's true that the little boy or girl you once were, you still are, how do we ever "grow up"?

The Little Boy or Girl You Once Were Can Grow Up!

It isn't always easy to begin looking deep into yourself, so congratulations! You've shown great courage by hanging in there with me this far.

Now it's up to you. There are two ways you can respond to this chapter.

The first is to hear those words "the little boy or girl you once were, you still are" as a proclamation from on high that you can't escape and you can't renegotiate.

If that's the message running through your head, I'd like to interrupt for a brief commercial announcement from your friendly neighborhood sponsor—me. The very fact that you believe you can't escape your past is evidence that you're believing the lie that you don't amount to much. If you believe that it's better to stay in Neverland, going in circles on the merry-go-round of your flawed private logic, you're still lying to yourself. Your natural tendency—if you don't fight it—is to return to the flawed private logic you learned as a child. But that is your propensity, not your destiny—the way your life could go, not the way your life will go. Even if your life story is a difficult one, you have a perfect opportunity to change course now as we explore your childhood memories. This book could even serve as a crucial reference point. But just how crucial this reference point proves to be in your life is up to you.

The other response you could have to this chapter is to believe the truth that you can change. You've told yourself lies—we all have—and now you're choosing to seek the truth that change is possible.

And it really is possible! I know that not only because I've seen it in the lives of thousands of people I've counseled and spoken to over the years, but also because I've seen it in my own life by confronting the lie that the little boy I once was—that rebellious little trickster—defines who I am today. Sure, I hear echoes of that little boy telling me which direction to go, but those little boy's echoes have grown farther and farther away as I've chosen to embrace the truth about the lies I told myself.

So where do we go from here? We'll continue moving forward by looking back to see why we remember what we remember, and just how you stored the key moments that make you *you*.

CHAPTER 3

Your Built-In "Aha!" Camera

Why you remember what you remember

All of us have done something we regret, whether it was a comment blurted out to a family member or an impulsively made decision that hurt a friend. Those moments may be the lowlights among the highlights we remember. When I look back on my childhood, sneaking a cigarette after school with the neighborhood rebel, Eddy, doesn't rank among my most shining moments. But there it is, stored away with the rest of my memories.

In the 1950s—as crazy as it seems in hindsight—smoking was "in." Everybody, it seemed, was doing it. Actors and actresses puffed away in movies and on television. One commercial campaign at the time even had athletes boasting that one brand of cigarette didn't "get your wind . . . you can smoke all you want!"[1] Just watching Humphrey Bogart movies will probably give you emphysema. And because I gravitated toward playing the rebel, one of my early childhood memories—yes, at only seven years old—involves my first experience with smoking.

I was walking to school one morning when I happened to see a brand-new, unsmoked Viceroy cigarette lying on the sidewalk. I couldn't believe my luck! I picked it up, put it in my pocket, and carried it with me all day at school like a secret.

Walking home after school that afternoon, I crossed paths with Eddy, our 12-year-old neighborhood troublemaker. My rebellious side longed to impress him, and because Eddie had a bike, I bummed a ride home with him. As I climbed onto his handlebars, I asked him as casually as if I were asking the time of day, "Hey, Eddy, got a light?"

Of course Eddy did have a light, so I left my parents' teaching on resisting peer pressure there on the sidewalk where I should have left the cigarette. Instead I lit up and smoked that baby all the way home, inhaling it with pride.

That's one incident I'm not too proud to have deposited into the Leman memory bank! If my tendency is to forget appointments without my assistant's help, why—of all the things I could remember in my childhood—do I remember sneaking that cigarette? If we forget the very things that we're supposed to remember—friends' and relatives' birthdays, chores and errands we promised we'd do, debit card PINs, Web site log-ins and passwords—then why do we remember specific early childhood memories out of the hundreds of thousands of possibilities? You might be surprised at the reason, because it doesn't necessarily have to do with whether or not your memories are dramatic.

In fact, all that's needed for you to hold on to a memory is an emotional spark—some catalyst to help store the experience into your brain's long-term memory.

And You Think Your Computer's Cool?

I'll be honest. I get as excited about computers as I do about colonoscopies. I simply don't have much use for them. (Computers, that is. At my age, I need the regular colon checks.) Oh, sure, from time to time I'll go online with my youngest daughter, Lauren, to see who she's chatting with and what they're talking about, but that's about it. I know that some people look forward to each new computer upgrade as if they were in Times Square waiting for the ball to drop on New Year's Eve. But me? I'll begin using our computer when I can toss it the keys to the car and have it drive me downtown to take care of the week's grocery shopping.

But when our friends began looking at the computer our kids used as if it belonged in a museum—which it probably did—Sande and I put our heads together and figured we'd better do something.

So after some biased, unscientific research consisting simply of calling our son, Kevin, for his advice, we bought our daughter Hannah an Apple iBook notebook computer for her sixteenth birthday, knowing she would soon use it for college.

Since that time, of course, the amount of memory in computers has increased—as it always does. Years ago, everyone talked about computers' hard-drive space in terms of bytes. Then it was megabytes. Now it's gigabytes. By the time you read this, who knows how many quadzillabytes your computer will have!

Still, scientists tell me—and I'm quite happy to take their word for it—that my brain outperforms even the best supercomputer. I'm not talking about performing specialized tasks, such as mathematical functions or analyzing chess moves. Any supercomputer will leave my head spinning on those tasks. And why waste my time on math, something I'm not very good at anyway? I'm talking about the human brain's ability to process billions of operations per second as it gathers information about the world around us, compared to a fraction of that number for the machine.[2]

That's great news—unbelievably great news—for a guy who was kicked out of fourth grade for a day for behavior problems and who was part of a reading group with kids who ate paste. If only I could have used that information in high school: "I know I flunked my last geometry test, Ms. Wilson. But as you calculate my grade, I think you should take into account the fact that my brain still outperforms the best supercomputer."

Our brains really are amazing organs because of what they help us remember. A single smell can pull all sorts of memories from my mental archives. I can still vividly picture those three concrete steps in front of our house in New York nearly sixty years later. But even more amazing is what the brain chooses to forget. Can you imagine what life would be like if we could remember in high-definition clarity every mistake we'd ever made? How awful would HD memory be?!

Instead, Almighty God made us in a wonderfully gracious way. He's given us minds more powerful than our best supercomputers, able to take in their surroundings in a fraction of a second, yet able to set aside so many of the things that we would rather forget. Sure, I remember events my mind knows I should—mistakes I shouldn't repeat, pain I never want to experience again, and ways that others have hurt me so that I can do my best never to be hurt that way again. But still my mind has a pretty convenient auto-delete function that allows me to put behind the things I've said to others that I immediately wish I could take back or things they've said to me. I sometimes delete things inadvertently, as everyone does, such as promises I make to Sande to do chores around the house. But all in all, the design for storing our long-term memories while forgetting the little slips we make along life's way is brilliant. Simply brilliant.

But just exactly how do we remember those long-ago childhood events?

Emotions—The Gateway to Long-Term Memories

Researchers are finding what I long suspected through decades of private practice—that the human brain stores long-term memories through our emotions. For us to store our memories for years, "we must either get information repeatedly or strongly," said an assistant professor at Wake Forest University Baptist Medical Center of the work that he and other researchers are performing. And "one of the hallmarks of memories that last is a close association with emotion."

> My mind has a pretty convenient auto-delete function.

Without dragging you into the biochemistry lab to bore you with the details of how enzymes build connections between the nerve cells that help us recall our memories, a hormone and neurotransmitter called norepinephrine provides the key to allow long-term memories into our memory vaults.[3] Imagine that you were somehow able to magically transport yourself back to the day when you had your first childhood memory—let's say that it was in preschool when you were only three years old. Perhaps it was the pain of smacking your head into another child's as you played tag outside. Perhaps it was the thrill of hearing the teacher praise you for being the only one in class to bring a show-and-tell object for letter *s* week. Perhaps it was directing the kids in how they should sit in a circle for a game of Duck Duck Goose. Whatever that experience was that resonated with who you are—that provided answers to the particular questions your psyche was asking—it triggered your body to release norepinephrine into your system, opening the vault door of your long-term memory. That memory was then stored away to be recalled later. For some, that key experience included a component of social interaction. For others, it included contemplation or solving puzzles.

For comedian Bill Murray, it involved making those closest to him laugh.

Bill Murray Went to Great Pains to Make Others Laugh

As a psychologist and a humorist besides, I love the movie *What About Bob?* Richard Dreyfuss plays Dr. Leo Marvin, a psychologist who confidently (and quite naïvely) takes on an extremely obsessive-compulsive patient named Bob. By the end of the movie Bob has driven Dr. Marvin crazy, and doctor and patient essentially switch roles.

Actor Bill Murray, who played the character Bob, grew up in a large Irish Catholic family, the fifth of nine children (seven brothers and one sister) in a household that Bill described as a "constant claustrophobic mess."[4] Though four of the siblings tried show business—"five if you insist on counting my sister, the nun, who does liturgical dance,"[5] points out Murray—Bill was the one who made it big by generating laughs on *Saturday Night Live* and then in such blockbuster movies as *Ghostbusters* and *Groundhog Day*. But even though making people laugh has long been an integral part of Bill's life, entertaining at home as he was growing up presented a different challenge.

"My father was a very difficult laugh," recalled Murray. "Adults found him very funny. But his children had a tough time cracking him up." Out of that challenge, however, emerged one of Bill's most telling childhood memories:

> One of my strongest childhood impressions is falling off my dinner table while doing a Jimmy Cagney impression. I hit my head very hard on the metal foot of the table leg, and it hurt terribly. But when I saw my father laughing, I laughed while crying at the same time. I guess that was some kind of beginning.[6]

Something inside Bill Murray, in spite of the intense pain of smacking his head against the metal table leg, caused him not to remember the pain so much as the victory of getting his father to laugh. That need to make people laugh—especially those dearest to him—is clearly central to Bill's private logic and created one of his most vivid early childhood memories.

In some ways Bill Murray's memory is very similar to my own memory of messing up the Williamsville Billies cheer—pain, followed by a much stronger sense of accomplishment at having made people laugh. It was during that moment of making others laugh in spite of the brief physical or emotional pain of embarrassment that we both, in essence, thought, *Eureka, baby! Now this is what life's all about!*

Snapping a Mental Photo

It's easy to flip through the pages of a *National Geographic* magazine and romanticize the lives of its photographers. A photo of a sunset behind Paris's Eiffel Tower sets us daydreaming about a work assignment in the lovely City of Lights. Or those wishing for a bit more action beyond life in an office cubicle might imagine tracking rare, elusive snow leopards in the Himalayan Mountains.

But romance and excitement are only a small part of that photographer's story. Sure, their job entails coming face-to-face with gorillas in the mist, but there's an equally important part of the job that isn't quite as exciting—waiting in that damp mist for hours for the sun to rise. Waiting for days for torrential rain to break and provide the right light conditions for the cover photo. Waiting for weeks in subzero temperatures for a fleeting glimpse of that snow leopard's rear end.

Not exactly what we imagine it to be, is it?

I bring that up because when you're a child making memories to be filed in your long-term memory bank, you're like that *National Geographic* photographer on safari. Throughout the mundane moments of life—especially during your early childhood—you are subconsciously trying to figure out what life is all about. Because this is such an important function in childhood, your psyche is constantly waiting and watching for the moment that makes sense of the world around you and your place in it. That moment might be successfully finishing a puzzle on the living-room coffee table by yourself or watching a large koi glide through the water under a bridge while you're holding your mother's hand. Whatever that key is to you—and each person's key truly is unique—your psyche recognizes it when it comes.

> Your psyche is constantly waiting and watching for the moment that makes sense of the world around you and your place in it.

When it does, it arrives the same way a photographer's heart begins to quicken as he sees that snow leopard pad along a nearby ridgeline and then pause, framed against the snowy, jagged peaks behind him. In that moment, for the photographer, the composition of the image, the lighting, and the interaction between the subject and landscape fit the story he was assigned to investigate. Everything comes together in one moment and click!

There are moments you experience as a child that fit your story, your own private logic. When you least expect it, everything you are seeing and experiencing resonates with who you inherently are and have been told you are through your family environment. Suddenly, your psyche thinks, *Eureka—this is it! This is what I've been trying to figure out!* And in that "aha" moment, your psyche essentially triggers that norepinephrine into your system, allowing you to take a mental photo and store it away in your long-term memory. For Bill Murray, that moment included a need to make others laugh so strong that even a throbbing headache didn't change it. It is as if that child on assignment, trying to figure out himself and the world around him, was hacking through the jungle of life and suddenly came face-to-face with the goal of his search. There it is! he thinks. The answer I've been searching for to who I am and what my role is in this world!

Click!

Emotions That Trigger Memories Need Not Be "Emotional"

"But if childhood memories are stored by my emotions," you may ask, "why then does it seem that my memories aren't all that emotional?"

In an interview, actor Denzel Washington was once asked, "What's the strangest thing that's ever happened to you?" Thinking back to one of his early childhood memories, Washington replied:

> When I was a child I thought I saw an angel. I woke up one night, and it had wings and kinda looked like my sister. I walked over to the door and opened the door so some light could come into the room, and it sort of faded away. I asked my mother about it, and she said it was probably my Guardian Angel. So I've always felt protected. It was as real as you are in front of me now; that's the God's honest truth.[7]

You would think that most of our childhood memories would be these kinds of dramatic events, the kind of memories that if strung together might look like a trailer for a gripping, blockbuster movie.

But interestingly that's rarely what we remember.

Even if a two-and-a-half-year-old releases the parking brake on the family minivan and it rolls down the street into the intersection during rush-hour traffic, or that same child somehow finds a way to wander inside the fence down the street to "play wid da doggies," a neighbor's pair of trained-to-kill rottweilers, chances are good that those will not be among that child's earliest memories, unless of course they tap directly into that child's private logic. Denzel Washington's dramatic memory of the angel in his room is definitely the exception to the rule.

Though the information in our long-term memories must come "repeatedly or strongly" for most of us, our early childhood memories are, well, rather mundane. Downright ordinary. The kind of event that could have happened hundreds of thousands of times. In fact, if you were to ask a group of people what their childhood memories are, you'd find that most people's memories aren't dramatic or even necessarily what we might term "emotional" at all. As you think back on your own childhood memories, you'll probably notice that, by and large, most of them aren't the kinds of things that we would choose to include if we were splicing together highlights from our lives.

When I talk about emotions triggering memories to be stored into the long-term memory vault, I'm not necessarily talking about extremely happy, sad, or even fearful memories. Just because norepinephrine is flowing to store those memories doesn't mean that they involve life-and-death experiences or the kind of experience that might trigger in you a fight-or-flight response.

All kinds of feelings can trigger your long-term memories. "Emotional" for you may be a sense of wonder. It may be curiosity. It may even be the feeling of security, a desire for others to care for you, or a compulsion to seize control of a situation. Whether you're an emotional person or not—whether you go all mushy at commercials for Puppy Chow or whether you watch stoically as your football team comes from behind to win the Super Bowl in the final seconds of the game—your memories are still emotional to you. Putting down the final piece of a puzzle of Yosemite National Park may be one of your most vivid early childhood memories. To you, finishing that puzzle mattered immensely—so much that your psyche opened your long-term memory vault and placed memories of that experience and your accompanying feeling inside for safekeeping.

That's what I love about your childhood memories and why you remember what you do—it provides a snapshot of who you are. No one else. Just you, without the psychological trappings that we all add as we grow older.

Some Things Are Just Meant to Be

TV talk-show host Larry King has interviewed over forty thousand people, including politicians, celebrities, athletes, and ordinary citizens thrust into extraordinary circumstances. Some might think that his start in radio, however, was a rather unlikely beginning to the career of one of today's most-recognized broadcasters. Listen to Larry tell the story of his first moment ever on radio:

> I go in, I sit down, cue my record up—Les Elgart, "Swinging Down the Lane"—and my hands are shaking. This is, by the way, the last time I was ever nervous, was that first day. And I'm really scared. Now I start the theme music. I turn on the microphone, I lower the theme music and nothing comes out. Nothing! I turn off the microphone; I turn up the record, and in that one minute of all you're hearing at home is a record being faded, I am realizing that I don't have the guts. In other words, I have everything else I wanted, but I don't have the chutzpah to say, "I'm a broadcaster." This was a pipe dream, and I really in that minute saw everything going away.

Marshall Simmonds—God rest him, he died last year—kicked open the door to the control room, and screamed, "This is a communications business! Communicate!" And he slammed the door. I did something then, almost 40 years ago, only 22 years old, that I still do now. I decided I had nothing to lose, so I was just myself.

I turned on the microphone, turned down the record and I said, "Good morning, this is my first day ever on radio. All my life I wanted to be in radio. I prayed for this moment. I was just given a new name. My name is Larry King. It's the first time I've ever said that name and I am scared to death. But the general manager just kicked open the door and he said that this is a communications business. So bear with me, I'm going to try to communicate." I never was nervous again.[8]

It took a lot of waiting, working, and dreaming for Larry to reach that point of sitting down in front of a microphone for the first time, but what propelled him throughout life to become one of the most famous interviewers was a seemingly innate desire to go into broadcasting. Listen to one of his early childhood memories:

When I was 5 years old I would lie in bed, look at the radio, and I wanted to be on the radio. I don't know why. I was magically attuned to it. I would listen to these voices, and then as I got a little older—and just a little older, 7 or 8—I would imagine myself doing what they were doing. I would actually stand up, sit down, I'd go to the mirror, and I would say, "The Romance of Helen Trent," as if I were the announcer. Then I would go to baseball games and I'd roll up the score card, and I'd sit up in the back row, and all my friends would look up at me, and I'd broadcast the game to myself. I fantasized being a broadcaster.[9]

Some themes that emerge in our childhood memories, it appears, suggest that aspects of our personalities were probably always with us in some way. Larry clearly aspired to be on the air from an early age, and doing something like broadcasting was probably part of his inherent makeup.

In other words, even if you were to grow up on a desert island without family, friends, or any other human contact, you would still develop interests based on who you inherently are—say, classifying the island's plants versus taming the howler monkeys for pets—which would be reflected in your childhood memories. Studies show that you can observe children's temperaments and activity in a nursery and then correlate their behavior closely to those kids' personalities later in life. A quiet child who is content to play with blocks by herself or read a book in the beanbag chair in the classroom corner will probably have more introspective memories. By her nature, she's very comfortable playing alone. Mr. Social Butterfly, however, must always be flitting from the preschool sandbox to the center of the ring-around-the-rosy game to the teacher to show off his newly perfected somersault technique.

I can certainly relate to both Bill Murray's and Larry King's memories, because I know what it's like to have that drive to make people laugh or comment over the airwaves—to feel it so strongly that it seems hardwired inside you. For Bill Murray, it was making people laugh. For Larry King, it was being on the air. For me, it's a little of both. I love cracking jokes on the air!

"So are these propensities formed by nature or nurture?" you ask. Everybody goes around and around on that question. I'll let you in on a secret: Both shape who we are.

How we are nurtured provides a whole other area to explore of why we remember what we remember. After all, what could be a more important influence on our memories than the people who've been around us the most, the people who have helped form who we are today—our families?

The members of your family—love 'em or leave 'em—have had a far more significant impact on you than you could imagine. And that impact didn't stop with your childhood either.

CHAPTER 4

The Apple Doesn't Fall Far from the Family Tree

Why you remember what you remember—take two

"So, Kevin, what are you speaking about?" my older sister, Sally, asked me one morning as the two of us enjoyed breakfast together.

It was an unusual day. Both of us were speaking at the same convention—she was presenting a workshop, and I was about to give the keynote address in 55 minutes.

"I haven't decided yet," I answered between bites.

I could almost see the color drain from her face as she mentally calculated the minutes before I was to step onstage in front of thousands of people.

"You're making my stomach turn," she said.

Sally knows from experience that her little brother is a joker par extraordinaire, so I can imagine that she was trying to read whether or not I was serious. But when I didn't show any sign of clowning around, she replied, "You really don't know what you're going to say?!"

"No," I told her matter-of-factly, "I really don't." I calmly took another bite of my breakfast.

I wasn't stretching the truth. I really didn't know what I was going to talk about. Planning every detail "so far" ahead of a talk simply isn't my style, though I realize that my approach makes my sister and a lot of other people I know sick to their stomachs. Sally would rather draft her entire talk with every word scripted, typed, and spell-checked weeks before. She's like a classical musician, practicing every note months ahead of her performance. I guess you could say I'm more like a jazz musician, preferring to feel the energy of the crowd and allowing conversations I have with people there to direct what I'll say on the spot.

If you're like me, you may find it fascinating that Sally and I both came from the same family, yet we have incredibly different ways of doing things. Why is that? If you have kids in your household or think back to your siblings as you grew up, you may have asked that question at one time or another. Perhaps the firstborn daughter in the family looks like she practically has the Nobel Peace Prize in her hands while the lastborn child acts as if he's aspiring to be a Mafia hit man.

In the last chapter, we talked about the innate qualities that play into your childhood memories. If you were raised by a pack of wolves, those might be the only factors that make you who you are. For most of us, though, one of the most significant factors influencing who you are and what you remember as a child is—you guessed it—your family. I've written a lot about the effect that parenting styles and birth order have on us in other books (*The Birth Order Book, Making Children Mind without Losing Yours,* and *Running the Rapids: Guiding Teenagers through the Turbulent Waters of Adolescence,* if you're interested in learning more). I often point out how interesting it is that all the cubs come out of the same den, yet every one is different and generally blazes a new trail as he or she goes out into the world.

In this chapter, then, I'd like to talk about how the *families* we grew up with influence our childhood memories, revealing who we were then—and who we are today.

Ad-libbing on the Family Stage

Have you ever played that game in which one person leaves the room and those remaining concoct a scenario that the person outside will be thrust into when she returns? When the person reenters the room, her goal is to figure out what her role is based on what everyone else in the room is saying and doing around her. She might be the coach of a football team during halftime of a championship game, a scientist who's just discovered the cure for cancer, or a reporter broadcasting live from a city being overtaken by Godzilla. But she doesn't know her role until she dives in, answering their questions, joining in the charade with the rest of the group, and trying her best to figure out what in the world is going on.

> Growing up in a family is a lot like stepping onto that stage in which everyone is ad-libbing.

Growing up in a family is a lot like stepping onto that stage in which everyone is ad-libbing. You have a part to play, but it's difficult to say at first exactly what it is because no one receives a script at birth. So you spend years figuring out what your role is without stepping on anyone else's toes. Every family has a different rulebook, and almost all of its rules are unspoken. For some families, a holiday meal together plays out like a rugby match, everyone talking at once and reaching over one another for the cranberry sauce and stuffing, and pounding the table at a good joke. For others, that same table on Thanksgiving is as quiet and orderly as if England's Queen Elizabeth were at the table. In still other families, you might never even dream of having a meal together at all because of the tension or because of emotionally absent family members.

Though every family's rulebook is different, we all share the same need to be loved and accepted by our family, to contribute to it in a way that helps us feel we belong, and to prove ourselves competent at something in life that sets us apart from our siblings. To accomplish this, we all strive for the attention of those who matter most in our lives—our parents. A child's innate drive to find a place in the hearts of her parents is as strong as her need to breathe. It's as if we're all born crying out, "Love me! Accept me! Help me fit in!" And to set

41

ourselves apart from "the competition"—our siblings—we learn to cut our own path. If the academic track is filled, we might try athletics. If the contemplative slot is filled, we might become the social butterfly. And if all of the seemingly available slots to receive positive attention appear filled, sometimes kids shift to negative attention-getting behavior to stand out.

Did you ever notice that very few siblings participate professionally in the same sport? There were the DiMaggio brothers—baseball star Joe DiMaggio and his two brothers. Today there are the Williams sisters in tennis—Venus and Serena—and the Manning brother quarterbacks—Peyton and Eli. But they're exceptions to the rule.

> We're all born crying out, "Love me!" "Accept me!" "Help me fit in!"

Because your birth order makes such a difference in who you are, let's consider how the different birth orders cause different themes in childhood memories.

Falling into Rank—Your Birth Order

Growing up in a family is a little like being born into a military hierarchy—you are always looking to the person above you to see how you're expected to conduct yourself. Firstborn and only children in a family look to their parents and the other adults around them for their cues; middleborn children look to that firstborn child and above; and the babies of the family have nowhere to look but up! As each of those children learn their roles in the family drama, certain patterns emerge according to their birth orders. (I've even coauthored a series of children's books with my son, Kevin II, tailored to each birth order: *My Firstborn, There's No One Like You*; *My Middle Child, There's No One Like You*; *My Only Child, There's No One Like You*; and *My Youngest, There's No One Like You.*)

Firstborns

If parents are the captains of the USS *Good Ship Family,* then the first-born child is like the first mate. For the firstborn child, there are no older brothers or sisters to take cues from on how to handle the first day of Cub Scouts, the first hour of violin lessons, or the first day of first grade. The firstborn child is forever faced with leading through a maze of firsts, with no one but adults towering above to show him how to blaze that trail. Consequently, firstborn children are much more likely to grow up more quickly than younger siblings and develop a deeper sense of responsibility because of the expectations upon them. And because all slots for parental recognition are open to the firstborn, by trial and error that child typically distinguishes himself in the most readily available proving ground—school.

43

Onlies

Only children exhibit similar patterns as firstborn children, but often to the extreme. Firstborns speed down the road toward adulthood faster than other birth orders, but only children often pass even firstborns. Why? Because onlies relate to adults almost exclusively. Also, apart from peer friendships, an only child isn't going to have nearly as many opportunities to solve interpersonal problems as a child with brothers and sisters typically works through on a daily basis. Consequently, an only child ends up with many traits common to the firstborn child—but magnified a few degrees—along with a greater familiarity with solitude, which often results in introspective memories.

Middleborns

Middleborn children, as you might imagine, often get overlooked in the middle. By the time the second or third child comes along in a family, every whimper from that child is not going to be attended to by the parents. And because they're sandwiched so neatly between the firstborn and lastborn children, they're often the children who are seen but not heard. Middleborns are masters of compromise and smoothing the waters of life. They are the kind of people who become great diplomats, able to see both sides of a position. Because they're in the middle, they are also the most difficult to categorize, as the middle child can be the second of three or the ninth of ten—and each of those children is probably going to experience significantly different family circumstances growing up.

Lastborns

Lastborn children—the babies of the family—are good at entertaining others, often seek to be the center of attention and the life of the party, and can wiggle their way into your heart through their charm. By the time the baby of the family comes bouncing along, the family has loosened up quite a bit. That baby now has a lot of modeling above her both in terms of older siblings and adults, and as she watches the older kids and tries to get a piece of Dad's and Mom's attention, she's quick to realize that most of the obvious avenues are taken—academics, athletics, etc. Consequently, the baby usually learns that the way to gain attention is by "working the crowd," fluttering her doe eyes to make even stoic, stodgy Uncle Stan coo at her.

This attention-getting behavior can also work against the baby when older brothers and sisters write her off, saying such things as, "Oh, don't pay attention to her." As the rest of the siblings see it, there's nothing that baby could say or do that should be taken seriously. But the baby of the family can rise to that challenge and develop an I'll-show-you attitude. People who told me that I'd never amount to much only served to make me try harder, so if there's a birth order that may lap those older siblings in the race of life, it can be the baby for that reason.

How do these birth orders affect our memories and the kind of persons we become? Because children of different birth orders develop different ways of conducting themselves, their memories also have different recurring themes.

Breaking the Rules, Making Mistakes, Falling Down

While most of us know Fred Rogers as the television host of *Mister Rogers' Neighborhood,* it may surprise you to know that he was also a Presbyterian minister and that he considered neither his work as a television host nor his pastoral ministry as the work nearest and dearest to his heart. Instead, it was his music that he felt was most central to who he was, and he composed over two hundred songs.[1] When you think about it, how can you separate Mister Rogers from his music? Is it possible to remember him coming through the front door of his television "home" and settling in by changing from his jacket into his trademark cardigan sweater (which incidentally now hangs in the Smithsonian Institution) without also hearing the words to his opening song running through your mind? *"It's a beautiful day in this neighborhood, a beautiful day for a neighbor. Would you be mine? Could you be mine?"*

His love of music clearly goes back his childhood:

> When he [Fred Rogers] was still a preschooler, his parents told him that he could choose anything he wanted from a toy catalogue. "When I saw the toy piano on one of the pages," Rogers remembers, "that was it! Now it seems to me that music has always been at the root of who I am and what I do."
>
> From that first toy piano, Rogers soon graduated to real instruments. His grandmother gave him an electric organ and by the time he was ready for school, he was entertaining people on a full-scale model. "Dad would put the speakers out on the front porch and people would drive up and down the street to hear me play. It was exciting, but I remember that I also worried about making mistakes."[2]

That is a very telling memory, for it not only reveals Fred's personal interest in music, which he recognized had "always been at the root of who I am and what I do." It also reveals a theme that you'll find

45

emerging in most firstborn and only children's memories—that even when Fred was playing the music he loved, he "also worried about making mistakes."

Because the firstborn child matures more quickly under a heightened sense of responsibility, he is more likely than other birth orders to have memories of stepping over those lines of responsibility either voluntarily or involuntarily. Memories that involve making mistakes, breaking rules, or getting hurt are very common for firstborn or only children. When I meet a firstborn or only child, in fact, I assume that they have a memory that touches on one of these related themes. A firstborn or only child's memories might be similar to Fred Rogers's memory and focus on an apprehensive first day in kindergarten. It might involve breaking one of Mother's china dishes in the kitchen or visiting the nurse's office after falling down on the playground blacktop and skinning a knee.

As he grew up, Fred Rogers decided to face his insecurities head-on. He went on to create a television show that helped children deal with the very same issues—learning proper self-esteem, handling feelings in appropriate ways, and receiving the message that you are valuable simply because of who you are.

Mister Rogers' Neighborhood made you want to sing, "It's such a good feeling, to know you're alive; *it's such a happy feeling, you're growing inside!*"

Minding the Details

Sande and I may as well admit it—we're both hooked on the TV show *24.* Perhaps the telltale clue was the comment we jokingly made to our kids, "Don't call us on Monday night!" I know that TV shouldn't be that important, but I'm telling you, Sande and I find ourselves glued to the set every week.

For those of you who aren't familiar with the series, each season follows one day—one blood-pressure-bursting day—in the life of LA's

Counter-Terrorist Unit, with agent Jack Bauer fighting for his life and just about everyone else's. It's nonstop action—a trip to the hospital takes about four minutes and no one has "gone potty" on *24* in five years. Talk about holding it! How could they go? There's simply no time! Each season is what I call one very stressful day at the office.

Do you wonder what kinds of things were running through the mind of actor Kiefer Sutherland, aka Jack Bauer, as a child? Though it's not technically an early childhood memory, listen to one of his memories of playing ice hockey:

> "I had my head down as I was crossing the blue line," he recalled of one game, "and I was looking for someone to pass to and I was looking the wrong way and I got hit by the biggest kid in the league. It knocked me out cold—I was about eleven or twelve—and I woke up on a stretcher and people were clapping, and I thought they were clapping because they were taking me out of the game and I started to cry.
>
> "My mother had to tell me later that they were clapping because I was still alive!"[3]

Kiefer's memory not only shows that classic firstborn theme of getting hurt (he has a twin sister who is six minutes younger, and three younger half brothers[4]), but it also appears to point to a personal theme of feeling unwanted or unwelcome. As he slips back into consciousness, he assumes that everybody is clapping because they're fed up with him and his hockey performance on the ice and are glad to get rid of him. Talk about the ever-striving private logic of a firstborn child! You'll also notice that Kiefer doesn't simply remember getting hit and regaining consciousness. He remembers where he was on the ice (the blue line), where he was looking at the time he was hit (down at the ice), and the fact that he was searching for someone on his team to pass to, as opposed to making a run with the puck himself. That level of detail often occurs in the memories of firstborn and only children.

I once spoke on birth order at a conference for accountants, which I imagine initially sounded about as interesting to them as a talk on accounting would have sounded to me. I could see it in their body language as I got up to speak. Their faces were stoic. Their arms were folded. Clearly they were not enthusiastic about the hour ahead of them.

So I went straight for the jugular.

Before even saying hi or introducing myself or thanking anybody in the room for inviting me, I blurted out, "If you were a firstborn child or an only child in your family, would you please stand?" About three hundred of them—nearly all of them in the room—stood. Even I was surprised at how many there were.

"Now, how many of you are middleborn children or the baby of your family?" About twenty of them raised their hands and I chuckled. "What are you doing here?!" I asked that group of twenty. Everyone laughed and leaned forward in their seats a bit, and I knew we were off to a great start.

My point is that firstborn and only children are the ones most likely to end up in jobs involving attention to detail, such as accountants and pilots. They're going to be the ones who get excited about clicking through the company's QuickBooks reports to find where every penny is going or tinkering with Linux computer code. Firstborn and only children—which account for almost all airline pilots—love charting a course to the hundredth of a degree and calculating the burn rate of fuel to the tenth of a gallon in relation to the weight of the airplane, taking into account the precise wind speed and its direction. Gather a cockpit full of lastborns and they'll more likely be tempted to think, *Forget wasting time on that navigation plan—let's get this party moving!*

I'll bet that if I would have sat down with those firstborn and only-born accountants after the conference for them to describe their childhood memories, you'd not only hear some of the themes we've talked about—mistakes, breaking rules, and getting hurt. You'd also hear detail after detail about what the crystal goblet looked like that he dropped or precisely what the weather was and what the full names were of those classmates who were beside him when he lost the sprint in first-grade PE. If you were a middleborn or baby of the family, as you listened you might think, *How in the world do you remember so much?* because firstborns and onlies generally remember much more detail in their memories than other birth orders.

What this detail in firstborns' and onlies' memories equates to is a drive to strive and achieve—in short, a propensity toward perfection. Firstborn children have no one to take their cues from except the adults above them, and it doesn't take keen observation to realize that adults are pretty good at coloring in the lines, tying their shoes, and cleaning their plates. Consequently, those children born first in the family also tend to be more impressed with authority, so they might have memories involving teachers, policemen, and other authority figures. On the flip side, those same children might have problems with authority because they've seen the hypocrisy in those who are supposed to be modeling healthy, appropriate authority.

There are plenty of exceptions to this rule about attention to detail, of course, so don't feel you need to turn around and walk out of the plane if you find that the pilot, copilot, and navigator on your next flight are all babies of their families. The cockpit flight crew probably won't work together like the Three Stooges, and they may very well fit some of the exceptions to this rule, which we'll talk about later in this chapter.

Surveying the Terrain and Moving Forward

There's never been any research that I know of to confirm this, but in my thirty years of private counseling work, my observation is that firstborn children often have what I call a "vertical component" and/ or "movement" in their memories. By this, I mean that a firstborn son or daughter in the family might have a childhood memory that involves standing on top of a mountain and looking out over a valley, or traveling in an elevator to the top of an office building and looking at the street below.

Why does he or she remember that? Because, once again, that particular incident is consistent with how that person views life. That doesn't mean he's supposed to take up mountain climbing or be a bellhop in the city, but it probably does mean that he's always striving, always climbing toward the top—which is certainly consistent with how many firstborns see life.

50

Another common feature of childhood memories for firstborns that's very closely related to the vertical component is movement—riding in a car or walking somewhere. Movement also translates into achievement, almost as if those firstborns or only children are running a race—which, if you are a firstborn yourself or think about your older brother or sister, you'll probably agree is true of the firstborn personality. Firstborns exhibit a pattern of striving and moving, looking down from where they've come or up to where they're going. Somehow achievement and movement are connected, and together these two form a common theme in firstborns' and only children's memories.

Kiefer Sutherland's memory of playing ice hockey is one example of movement. Here's another. Steven Spielberg—director of such movies as *Close Encounters of the Third Kind*, *E.T.*, and *Schindler's List*—once shared about his childhood in Phoenix, Arizona, with film critic Roger Ebert:

> My dad took me out to see a meteor shower when I was a little kid, and it was scary for me because he woke me up in the middle of the night. My heart was beating; I didn't know what he wanted to do. He wouldn't tell me, and he put me in the car and we went off, and I saw all these people lying on blankets, looking up at the sky. And my dad spread out a blanket. We lay down and looked at

the sky, and I saw for the first time all these meteors. What scared me was being awakened in the middle of the night and taken somewhere without being told where. But what didn't scare me, but was very soothing, was watching this cosmic meteor shower. And I think from that moment on, I never looked at the sky and thought it was a bad place.[5]

That is another classic firstborn child's memory with both the movement in the car and the fascination with looking into the night sky at the meteor shower. Spielberg's memory also has the element of fear that we talked about, which is characteristic of responsible firstborns and only children. "What is going to happen to me?" little Stevie wondered.

This experience obviously made a great impression on him, and as Roger Ebert points out later in the interview, the image of light (the meteors) as the source of mystery appears in many of Spielberg's films as his "master image," as Ebert calls it. Light from the UFO in *Close Encounters of the Third Kind* conceals the unknown, and the blinding Nazi spotlights in the *Indiana Jones* movies conceal an unknown threat.

"Don't worry," I wish I could have told young Spielberg. "You're generating material for future blockbuster movies."

Lonely Onlies

Whenever I see someone seated next to me on an airplane doing a crossword puzzle, I assume that I'm sitting next to a firstborn or an only child. Nine times out of ten I'm right.

Both firstborn and only children love words and figuring things out, and because they've each lived for a time without siblings they are more likely than other birth orders to have introspective memories. That familiarity with solitude, however, is true especially of the only child. A few things might distinguish an only child's memories from a firstborn child's memories, such as memories of being by herself, even if she spent a fair amount of time with her parents, or the fear of being left alone. The kind of question that might run through an only child's private logic is, *What happens if Dad or Mom is in an accident and I'm all alone?*

Because of only children's familiarity with solitude and the fact that they are also good at structuring things, their memories will also be more likely than those of other birth orders to focus on interacting with things rather than people. Classic memories of an only child might involve solving a puzzle, putting the finishing touches on a woodworking project, or assembling the furniture in a dollhouse. Mathematics, music, engineering, or scientific endeavors would all be strong suits of an only child later in life because of their inclination to solve problems.

That isn't to say that only children won't have memories with people in them—that all depends on whether people are important to that person's private logic. Also, because only children grow up so quickly they're not going to have many memories of acting as a leader. They become leaders later in life, fiercely independent leaders as they distinguish themselves. But they haven't had as much practice in leadership as a firstborn child who exercises some reign over his or her younger siblings.

Unlike the middleborn or baby of the family, the only child by definition simply doesn't have the social practice that other birth-order children do.

Caught in Between

My brother, Jack, has always jokingly given me grief because, as the baby brat of the family, I was the one who got the new bike for my birthday. Not him—me. He wanted it, and I got it.

I can still remember that day. I was so happy when my parents gave it to me that I immediately went cruising around the neighborhood.

The only problem was that my party guests were still there. I'd left them to twirl their party hats and didn't return for a good half hour. That sort of behavior doesn't go over very well with anyone—parents or party guests—and it certainly didn't go over well with my middle-born brother who never got his own new bike.

His reaction wasn't a product of my personality or his own personality or even favoritism by our parents, so much as it was the fact that our parents, John and May Leman, were simply reenacting a pattern that families have followed for thousands of years. When the first child enters onto the family stage, all of the house spotlights are turned on him or her, the mics and speakers are amped up, and Dad and Mom—the audience—are tuned in to every word and cry. As you can imagine, my sister, Sally, received that kind of undivided attention from my parents. But by the time Jack came along three and a half years later, my parents had learned that eating dirt doesn't necessitate a call to the paramedics and that kids had a way of turning out all right even if you don't bronze their first pair of shoes or fill their baby scrapbooks with locks of hair from their first haircut. Consequently, middleborn children are going to recall childhood memories in which they are the mediator, the negotiator, or the compromiser. They'll also have memories of comparisons, memories of situations that felt unjust—such as my brother's childhood memory of me and my new bike.

Sorry, Jack. I guess that's sometimes the way the cookie crumbles for the baby of the family.

Party Time!

As you've gathered from my childhood memories, the baby of the family tends to remember being the center of attention, getting his way (or trying and failing!), and generally enjoying a good time. Remember, the baby takes his cues not only from the adults above him, but also from his siblings above—and children approach life much less seriously than adults. Consequently, babies of the family are likely to have childhood memories that involve birthday parties and holidays, gifts, or moments in which they're the center of attention. Look back at my memories and you'll discover some of the themes of the baby of the family—being the center of attention as I did my Williamsville Billies cheer, not getting my way when I was locked outside, and riding my new bike around the neighborhood during my birthday party.

Years later, while I was on the road speaking, I walked outside after breakfast and found that I was only a few blocks from the studios of ABC's *Good Morning America*, which I was a part of during the mid-1990s as their consulting psychologist when Charlie Gibson and Joan Lunden hosted the show. I soon found myself standing in a crowd peering through the window to their live set.

At that moment the show's floor director, Eddie Luisi, saw me in the crowd and did a double take. *Kevin?* he mouthed from behind the glass. He waved me around to the side door, whisked me through security, and within seconds I was standing on the live set of *Good Morning America* in my grubby shorts, NBC T-shirt, and Arizona Wildcats baseball cap that rarely leaves my head when I'm relaxing. The floor crew gathered around to say hi, then Eddie ushered me to the set desk with only five minutes until they went live. Charlie Gibson, one of my favorite people, greeted me with an emotional bear hug while Diane Sawyer stood there as if trying to figure out exactly who this unshaven person who had just walked in off the street was. The show's executive producer, Ben Sherwood, walked briskly up to the desk and looked around as if to say, H-e-l-l-o, we have a show to do here! I knew from experience what that look meant and quickly backed off.

"Hey, Kevin, don't leave yet!" Charlie shouted across the room as he settled behind his desk. Later, during a break in the broadcast, he introduced me to the rest of the crew.

I tell that story to illustrate the point that fun-loving, social babies of the family often see the world as one big, extended family. I'm in good company. Here's a list of lastborns you might recognize: Billy

Crystal, Eddie Murphy, Goldie Hawn, Drew Carey, Jim Carrey, Martin Short, Chevy Chase, Steve Martin, Whoopi Goldberg, Ellen DeGeneres, Steve Carell, Jon Stewart, Leslie Nielsen, the late John Candy, and the grandfather of all comedians, Charlie Chaplin. All of them are babies of their families. It's clear from this list that babies use their ability to draw attention to themselves not only as a lifestyle but also to make a living!

When Roles Are Reversed

Awhile back I mentioned that psychology is the science of recognizing patterns in human behavior, and from everything I've told you so far about birth order and memories, perhaps you have recognized what appear to be exceptions to the themes above in your own memories or in the memories of those you know.

I heard of one childhood memory from the baby of four children, for example, which occurred when he was five. He was at the mall when he saw a young girl taking money out of the courtyard fountain. He walked up to her and told her that she wasn't supposed to do that, but she didn't listen and went right on pulling pennies, nickels, dimes, and quarters from the water. So what did that lastborn child of the family do? He pushed her in!

You would be correct to conclude that that story, which touches on the theme of breaking rules, would be more likely to come from a firstborn or only child than from a baby. Unless, of course, there is at least a five-year gap between that lastborn child and the next oldest child.

Television host Jay Leno, for example, has been shaped by this five-year gap. He joined NBC history when he took over for Johnny Carson as the host of one of America's longest-running late-night talk shows, *The Tonight Show*, which has been running since 1954. Good choice, I'd say. Because along with Leno's experience as a stand-up comedian, I would add that his birth order makes him well-suited to host the show.

Leno was the lastborn of two boys—the large-chinned baby of the family. As you might expect, Leno had many traits common to babies of the family during his childhood, such as his love of humor. In fact, the story is often told of Jay's fifth-grade report card, on which his teacher had included the comment, "If Jay spent as much time studying as he does trying to be a comedian, he'd be a big star."[6] Little did Jay's fifth-grade teacher know that what set Jay apart back then would prove to be the very thing that set him apart and made him famous later in life.

But Leno was also ten years younger than his brother, Patrick.[7] So while Jay is technically the baby of the family, he also has some firstborn traits because of that large age gap between him and his older brother. Consequently, notice that one of his early childhood memories combines traits that you would find common to both babies' and firstborn children's memories—being the life of the party and getting hurt, all in one experience!

> One night in New Rochelle, my parents were having what I thought was a huge party, but I guess it was just two other couples over playing bridge. I had gone up to bed, but I'd crept back to the top of the stairs to eavesdrop on the party below. They were talking and laughing and having a good time, and I wanted so badly to be down there where the action was. So I hatched a plan: I would make a big showbiz entrance! I would slide down the banister in my pajamas, hit the bottom, land on my feet, and go, "Ta daaaa!" Right in the middle of the bridge game! I'd be the life of the party! Cause a sensation! Be like Liza Minnelli—who, of course, would have been about eight at the time, but still no doubt a load of excitement.
>
> So I balanced myself on the top of the banister and slid approximately one inch. And that was it. Suddenly, I fell like a nuclear missile—straight through a table with a lamp on it. There

was a huge crash as the table collapsed and the lamp shattered. Everybody jumped up from the card game, scared out of their minds. But what an entrance! My parents rushed me to the hospital, where my spleen had to be removed. Which was so cool to me at the time—well worth giving up an insignificant body part. I've never really missed my spleen, anyway.[8]

Jay's childhood memory is a perfect blend of the baby's fun-loving style and the firstborn's preoccupation with mistakes and getting hurt. Anybody who remembers losing his spleen and cracks jokes about it would lead me to believe he might be the baby of the family with at least a five-year age gap!

Donald Trump, the New York real-estate magnate, is another person who has experienced the role reversal of birth order in his family as he grew up. Trump was the fourth of five children, and naturally it was his brother, Freddie, the firstborn of the family, who was expected to take over the family business when he was old enough. But their personalities caused them to flip-flop.

> As a kid, I was making a building with blocks in our playroom. I didn't have enough. So I asked my younger brother, Robert, if I could borrow some of his. He said, "Okay, but you have to give them back when you're done." I used all of my blocks, then all of his blocks, and when I was done I had a great building, which I then glued together. Robert never did get those blocks back.[9]

Even though Donald was a middleborn child, he came to replace his complacent older brother, Freddie, as the mover and shaker of the family. In fact, moving and shaking wasn't all that Donald did.

"In the second grade," Donald Trump once recalled, "I punched my music teacher. Because I didn't think he knew much about music. . . . I'm not proud of that," Trump admitted, "but it's clear that early on I had a tendency to stand up."[10]

It was Donald Trump's "tendency to stand up" that not only caused him to switch birth-order traits with his oldest brother; it also led him to become one of the wealthiest men in the world with his New York real-estate holdings.

You can't assume that just because you're the second child of three that your memories are going to exhibit typical middle-child themes. Oh, I'm not disputing the fact that you are the secondborn child in your family, but you might still also be the firstborn son or daughter. Even if you have four older sisters and you're the fifth-born child who happens to be the firstborn boy, you'll probably take on some first-born characteristics because as you look up to those above you, you aren't going to see anyone to take your cues from on what it means to be a male until you reach your father. Conversely, if a firstborn child is physically or mentally challenged, he or she can shift birth-order traits with the next child down the line, so that if the firstborn boy in a family of two sons has a disability, that might cause the secondborn boy to adopt firstborn characteristics.

But birth order certainly isn't the only factor that influences who we are and the events we remember—your parents' parenting style also shaped you and your childhood memories immensely.

Were You Threatened with the "Shillelagh"?

If you shadowed my father and all three of his brothers throughout the day—even if you didn't know they were related—you'd agree by day's end that the four were all cast from the same mold. That's partly because they all grew up in a traditional authoritarian household in which my grandfather's word was absolute. He ruled not only in word but also in deed. And so, like father, like son, my own father was a hardworking man who ruled at times by threatening us kids. Over the years, I came to live in fear of what he called the "shillelagh."

Threatening me with the shillelagh was all it took to reform me

Memory Themes by Birth Order

	COMMON THEMES	POSSIBLE MEANINGS
Firstborns and only children	Breaking rules, making mistakes, getting hurt	Heightened sense of responsibility and consequences—and stepping over those lines either voluntarily or involuntarily
	Plenty of detail in the memories themselves	Propensity toward perfectionism—"getting the details right," so to speak
	Surveying a view from a height, looking up or down, moving somewhere in the memory	Achievement—being on the move to make things happen! Always pursuing excellence
Only children	Perfectionist memories, often without anyone else in them	Fierce independence because they naturally spend a lot of time by themselves
	Fearful memories	Often fear being left alone
Middleborns	Memories of comparisons	Competition with a capital C
	Memories of situations that felt unjust	A drive to right wrongs or at least to negotiate a balance that is beneficial to both parties
Lastborns	Memories often set around parties, holidays, or celebrations	Tend to be fun-loving, social people
	Memories of being the center of attention	

on the spot. If I was out of line he'd raise his voice, "Do you want me to get the shillelagh?"

"Oh, no—please don't get the shillelagh!" I'd say. "Anything but the shillelagh."

But with God as my witness, I had not the slightest clue what the shillelagh was.[11] I imagined some instrument handed down from the Middle Ages, generation after generation, by some secret society of parents devoted to the unyielding discipline of their children. Whatever the shillelagh was, I didn't want to find out! I realized years later, as an adult, that he never had a shillelagh.

Did you grow up in fear of the shillelagh? Did you live in a home where the fear of punishment kept you in line—or relatively close to it? Or did you live in a home where discipline was so laissez-faire that you and your siblings could easily overturn the parental establishment like a group of rioting, angry villagers with torches and pitchforks?

I bring this up because, in addition to birth order, one of the most important factors that shapes your childhood memories and who you are today is the parenting style that your parents used in raising you.

> One of the most important factors that shapes your childhood memories and who you are today is the parenting style that your parents used in raising you.

The permissive parent says in that singsong voice, "Tyler, it's eight o'clock. Have you chosen to get ready for bed yet?" Too many parents stumble all over themselves to make sure their kids never have any bad feelings toward them. Perhaps they grew up in authoritarian homes themselves, so they endeavor to create a "different environment" that's about as free-form as an anarchist's family.

At the other extreme, an authoritarian parent will say, "Tyler, if you aren't in that bed in five seconds, I'm going to show you the meaning of sorry!" That kind of parent doesn't believe that her child is capable of respecting healthy boundaries, so she does all she can to maintain "a clear and present danger" to her children. But that's not parenting. That's dictatorship.

The authoritative parent, however, says, "Tyler, I've told you that it's time for bed. If you decide not to listen, that's your choice. But there will be consequences." The authoritative parent sets healthy boundaries appropriate to her child's development, boundaries that give her child safe structure, that help set him up for success by placing proper responsibility on his shoulders, and that help him learn discipline from the inside out.

61

Whatever parenting style you grew up with, it will shape the childhood memories you have, whether the experiences and accompanying feelings in your memories reveal fear for always trying to measure up to impossible expectations or a desperate yearning for boundaries in a chaotic household.

How Family Circumstances Shape Your Memories

Whether you grew up under permissive, authoritarian, or authoritative parents, your private logic will also have been affected by any number of family circumstances, such as a tight or carefree financial situation, life-and-death health issues, frequent moves, etc. The list of possible circumstances influencing your memories is almost endless, but your childhood memories can help pinpoint which ones you were naturally sensitive to.

One of my childhood memories involved dashing down the stairs on Christmas morning, looking across the room, and seeing under the Christmas tree the blue football helmet with the yellow stripe down the middle that I had worn out God's ears praying for. My first thought was, *Oh, my goodness—I got the helmet I wanted!* But following immediately on the heels of the first thought was, *But I know my parents don't have money for that.* Does it take a PhD in psychology to assess that in our family money was tight, and that that same attitude toward money still remains in my life today?

Even now, when I'm on the road for business, that frugal voice inside my head still has me nickel-and-diming myself. I was in Atlanta a few years ago on the publisher's expense when I found that I could save money by taking a train that would drop me close to the downtown Atlanta Convention Center. So I took the train at $1.75 rather than the private car they had planned to send. My action was simply a function of that private logic from my childhood. (But just explain that to the befuddled publisher who was trying to figure out what I had done.)

Then, during one recent stay in New York to appear on a show, I took one look at the hotel breakfast menu and walked out because I couldn't bring myself to pay $36 for breakfast. Unlike my youngest kids, I don't exactly relish a visit to that fine Scottish restaurant—McDonald's. But I wandered down the street and into the Golden Arches for a heat-lamp-warmed, wax-paper-wrapped breakfast because my private logic was dictating to me in no uncertain terms that I could not do otherwise.

Truth be told, I was just following the lessons I'd learned from my parents. For years, the rest of the family used to jokingly remind my mother of her oft-repeated reminder to all us kids to get off the phone because a call cost "15 cents per minute to Grand Island!" My private logic, shaped by my family's financial situation and engrained in my childhood memories, still echoes in my decisions today.

There is no doubt that all of us are a product of our environment in so many ways. If money was also a stress to your parents, that may be part of your memories and private logic today as well. If you grew up in a military family and were bounced around the country every two years, that's going to affect how you view stability. Depending on how your private logic was formed, you may also find yourself having a difficult time putting down roots in any one place. Or you may shift to the other extreme and come to view a stable community as a man crawling through the desert views water.

A child living with parents who are easygoing circus performers is going to have significantly different childhood memories than someone living with parents who are part of an established, politically ambitious family. Listen to Ted Kennedy describe in his own words what it was like growing up in the Kennedy family:

> One of my most vivid childhood memories is of our family gatherings around the table at dinnertime. Conversation was lively and interesting, prompted by questions from my mother and father about events of the day. With nine of us eager to impress our parents as well as one another, it was hard to get a word in unless you had something interesting to say. We learned early that the way to be an active part of dinner conversation was to have read a book, to have learned something new in school, or, as we got older, to have traveled to new places. Our parents opened our nine young minds to the world that way, and it's been a wonderful lifelong gift.[12]

And every family's circumstance, like every person's private logic, is unique.

The Hazards of Perfect Laundry

Of all the family influences that shape our childhood memories, our private logic, and ultimately, who we are growing up, what I call the "critical-eyed parent" has a widespread detrimental effect on so many adult children I talk to today.

A woman once shared with me one of her early childhood memories in which she received all kinds of hassle from her parents because she wasn't folding the family's laundry correctly. To her parents, there was an undeniably correct way to fold towels, underwear, and socks. And doing otherwise was tantamount to criminal activity.

Perhaps there is a correct way to fold underwear. I don't know—I haven't read the *Underwear Folder's Handbook*. But even if Ms. Manners has an unyielding stance on the folding of underwear and all the etiquette guides are in complete agreement on how socks should be placed in your drawer, who really cares?! Do you really want to emphasize to your own flesh and blood that how she folds her underwear is more important than the fact that she's working hard, honoring you by her obedience, and contributing to the family? Are you really going to feel like a successful parent if you've raised an acid-bitter woman, venomous to others and estranged from you, her parent—but, oh boy, can she ever fold a mean pair of underwear!

64

What happens to children of critical-eyed parents is that they begin avoiding criticism at all costs because it becomes too threatening. Rather than finish a task, they'll stop an inch short and start something else.

Why? you wonder.

Imagine Ralph, whose office at the aerospace engineering firm looks like he set it up with help from the firm's wind tunnel. He's a procrastinator and his misguided mind-set is that by putting tasks off indefinitely, people can't tell him that he isn't doing his job well— because he's not finished! Sure, there's some order within his disorder, because if the boss came in and asked him for a file, he could probably find it. But to the naked eye, his office is a pigsty. Ralph is the sort of chap who grew up with a critical-eyed parent, and one of the ways he runs from his private logic of always needing to measure up to impossibly high personal standards is to perpetually put off stepping toward success.

Ralph is what I call a "defeated perfectionist," which is just one of the lifestyles that emerges from the many influences—both your natural, innate traits and the family environment you grew up in—that combine to create your childhood memories.

But what exactly is your lifestyle? That's the subject of our next chapter.

CHAPTER 5

Your Lifestyle Has Nothing to Do with the Car You Drive

When do you count in life?

Anybody who's ever waited in line at a Department of Motor Vehicles licensing office knows that such an experience doesn't usually make the end-of-the-year Christmas letter highlights. If there's one thing I dislike even more than working with numbers for hours on end, it's filling out long-winded bureaucratic forms.

But just leave it to a baby of the family to find a way around that awful task with his charm!

Now, whenever I go into the DMV office in New York, I bring the ladies who work there a homemade pie for their coffee break—a red raspberry pie, a blueberry pie, or a Dutch apple pie. In turn, they graciously fill out all my forms. Who wouldn't go out of their way for one of those? I know, because I've eaten more than my share! Call me a scheming little schnookie, but I look at the situation this way: A pie is a small token for the profound gratitude I feel for having been rescued from mind-numbing boredom.

It's not the first time I've done everything in my power to brighten up the mundane details of my day.

Because I fly so many miles for business, rather than call American Airlines' 1-800 number and discuss seating assignments and travel plans over the phone with a complete stranger seven states away, I used to simply drop by their local office here in Tucson. One day, when I was there making arrangements, somehow we began talking about this

65

bread called Milton's that I was absolutely crazy about. With the exception of hamburger buns, I don't get excited about eating anything that advertises seeds as its selling point. They're truly for the birds! Milton's bread, however, with its cracked wheat and a smattering of seeds on top makes, hands down, the best toast you've ever had in your life!

"You'll have to bring us some one day," they said.

"Okay," I replied, "I will."

Well, true to my word, that day came, and the next time I had business to take care of at that American Airlines office, I walked in with a toaster under my arm, a pound of butter, a knife, Milton's bread, and some napkins and paper plates.

"It's party time!" I announced as I entered. "Just show me to an outlet."

Soon I had my souped-up, four-slice, turbocharged toaster popping out toast as fast as we all could eat it. I was slathering fresh butter on those slices, and soon that American Airlines office smelled like mealtime at a bed-and-breakfast! The office workers were eating it up, and I was even handing out slices to customers who walked in, as if I were running the sample table at the local grocery store.

Well, too much of a good thing was indeed too much, because it wasn't long before my toaster blew the circuit! Because the American Airlines office was located in the front part of the Doubletree Hotel, a couple of seconds later a man walked in from the hotel.

"Do you have any power?" he asked, perplexed.

It turns out that they'd lost their power as well over my turbocharged toaster! As if that weren't enough, someone else from the Doubletree office walked quickly into the room.

"Does anybody else smell smoke?" he asked.

Apparently, when I pulled out one of those pieces of Milton's toast, part of it broke off in the toaster, and it started smoking like a fire department training burn!

Now I know that you probably don't carry a toaster with you on errands around town, but I like to mix it up, bringing a bit of a party wherever I am. I also know my off-the-wall behavior had grown in part out of my insecurity from treading in the footsteps of my "perfect" sister and near-perfect brother. As the fun-loving baby of the family, that's all part of the lifestyle that I've developed over the years.

What's *Your* Lifestyle?

As I was leaving the doctor's office after my last visit, I overheard one of the staff members say to a colleague, "Don't you just love it when he comes in here?" Perhaps they'd been talking about one of my previous visits when I'd made NASCAR racing-car noises as my doctor performed my colon exam. Again, I realize that's not the way everyone handles that sort of thing, but the way I look at it, you might as well make the best of an uncomfortable situation!

67

That is the way I look at every situation—to make the best of it by trying to get people to laugh. I'm the kind of guy who would be thrilled if my local bank gave away free door prizes every day of the year just for coming in and if all my trips to the grocery store turned into Broadway musicals featuring kumquat-juggling produce stockers and harmonizing checkout clerks. And I do all I can to help make those dreams a reality.

Those moments in the Department of Motor Vehicles licensing office, the American Airlines office, and my doctor's office have everything to do with my private logic, the lens through which I see life. And the expression of my strong, innate desire to make people laugh, that outworking of my inner reason in my day-to-day life, is what I call my "lifestyle."

Everyone has a different lifestyle—and I'm not talking about the kind of car you drive or how many square feet your house is. That's your standard of living. Your lifestyle is the pattern you establish throughout your life of how you respond to people and situations around you, what assumptions you make about yourself and your environment, and when your emotions kick in involuntarily.

Do you want to know what your lifestyle is? How would you complete the phrase "I feel that I matter in life when . . ."?

When Do You Matter?

As you step onto your family stage, it doesn't take long before you begin trying to figure out what role you've been handed. But eventually you learn how to get the attention you crave and you go for it!

> Do you want to know what *your* lifestyle is? How would you complete the phrase "I feel that I matter in life when . . ."?

Imagine little four-year-old Tyler's first week of preschool. When his mother drops him off the second day, he walks into the room and immediately begins bullying Grace for control of the overstuffed chair in the reading corner. Knowing from day one that Tyler can be a little split atom of energy, the teacher gently redirects him to the sandbox, which he loved the previous day when all the boys were playing there. But when he sees Scott playing with the only hammer next to him at the play woodworking bench, he sets his sights on that and tries to wrestle it from the poor tyke. It seems that Tyler seeks trouble wherever he turns.

Did you ever wonder why some children will enter a classroom and turn the other children against them in a matter of minutes? Some kids not only invite trouble—they seem to seek it.

Seeking trouble may be exactly what he's doing. As strange as it may sound, Tyler may be doing that because he's only comfortable in an uncomfortable situation. Perhaps life at home is turbulent and devoid of the positive love and attention he needs, so he's become accustomed to living in chaos and seeking negative attention. Children are adaptable, but if you place a child who's used to an unstable environment in a stable one, he's going to feel out of place because that stability does not feel "at home."

You may be the most loving preschool teacher in the world, but chances are that child will initially reject that love because being loved is inconsistent with how he views life at home. In fact, when he sees people trusting each other in that preschool classroom he'll be inclined to think, *What's wrong with you people? Don't you see that you're going about this all wrong?! If I am ever going to get people's attention, I need to get it however I can. Hmmm . . . getting into trouble seems to work nicely.* In other words, the message running through his psyche is I only count in life when I receive negative attention.

You, too, have a lifestyle that you've come to accept over the years of growing up. Part of my lifestyle could be phrased as "I only count in life when I make people laugh." And because certain lifestyle patterns emerge according to what order you were born into your family, for the firstborn or only child those lifestyles often are "I only matter in life when I control, dominate, or win." For the middleborn child, they are "I only count in life when I avoid conflict, keep the peace, or maintain a social balance so that everybody's happy." And for the baby of the family, those lifestyles often are "I only count when I'm the center of attention, when I'm able to put people in my service, or when I get my way."

But your own unique pattern of expressing your private logic, of course, doesn't mean that you're subject to that pattern forever. As you recognize what lifestyle you naturally fall into, you can learn to adapt your lifestyle thinking and even change patterns that negatively influence you and others.

Take Charge of Your Lifestyle!

If you've ever gone on a diet or started an exercise regimen, then you know the hard work that's involved. It takes vigilance to recognize that slippery slope down to your old patterns and to ascend toward the high ground of new ones. If you're trying to lose weight, you might set a routine of getting up early—often way too early!— to make it

69

to the gym before the day shifts into high gear. Otherwise you know that you aren't likely to exercise after work. You're too tired by then. If you're dieting, you're wise to pass by the donuts in the grocery store aisle—even if it does seem like they're calling your name.

Is it worth all the hassle?

Just ask someone who has gone through the rigor and succeeded at losing weight or toning up. Invariably it seems that person will tell you just how important changing his habits was to his health and well-being.

The same is true of making changes to your lifestyle. It's natural to stay—and want to stay—in the role that you've adopted growing up. If you're a pleaser, it's much easier to keep on pleasing others day after day, year after year. Of course, all this pleasing will eventually take its toll on your mind and body—your sanity and state of physical exhaustion. But what a difference it makes when you're able to hold to the strengths of your lifestyle and shed its weaknesses!

> It's natural to stay—and want to stay—in the role that you've adopted growing up.

As we discuss the lifestyle that has emerged from your childhood memories, it may feel a bit like looking in a mirror that reflects not only your outside but also your inside. Perhaps as you look at your birth order and your parents' parenting style, you may begin to realize that you need to make some significant changes to the way you look at yourself, others, and the world around you.

That's great—you're on the right path, heading in the right direction, and you can make it! Just because you find yourself resonating with a particular lifestyle that I describe doesn't mean that's who you'll be forever. Your lifestyle is only the foundation upon which you make your decisions and respond to situations around you. So don't believe the lie that you only matter when you're doing what comes naturally

70

to you. By consciously being aware of your lifestyle—the inherent strengths and weaknesses in how you respond to others and the world around you—you can make significant changes.

It takes time and grace to think differently, but with the help of Almighty God you can do it!

Are You on a Mission?

I once interviewed the Orlando Magic basketball team's senior vice president, Pat Williams, for a book I was doing. "Kevin," he told me, "when I get up in the morning and my feet hit the floor, I tell myself, 'I have to win.'"

If you're looking for a description of the private logic behind the lifestyle of a driver, there's no better description than that. A driver's internal mechanism starts when the alarm clock rings and runs all day.

A driver believes, *I only count in life when I'm moving forward.*

> A driver believes, *I only count in life when I'm moving forward.*

There are real benefits to that lifestyle, of course. Drivers don't sit around twiddling their thumbs, waiting for others to hand them the world on a silver platter. They are the ones most likely to get things done around the house, in your community of faith, or at the office. People come to count on drivers to finish tasks, and drivers receive plenty of praise for their lifestyle. The person who is always striving to get ahead in life very often will rapidly climb the ladder of success.

Oprah Winfrey apparently skipped kindergarten when her teacher received a letter at the beginning of the school year suggesting in no uncertain terms that Oprah should proceed straight into first grade. The teacher agreed. And perhaps it's a good thing that Oprah skipped ahead—because it turned out that it was Oprah who wrote the letter![1] Her drive is still evident today in practically everything she does. In the first movie she appeared in, *The Color Purple*, she received an

Academy Award nomination for her performance, and her company, Harpo Productions, has done pretty well . . . to put it mildly. I suspect that she's one of the wealthiest and most powerful women in the world, and you don't rise to that height without being a driver.

No pun intended, but do you think professional golfer Tiger Woods is a driver? He was once asked in an interview, "I'm curious if you can recall the first time you ever won a golf tournament or brought a trophy home."

> "Oh, yeah," Tiger replied. "I remember that. . . . I was about four years old, and I played in a pitch, putt and drive for little peewees. It was a 10-and-under deal, and I finished 2nd. I just remember the trophy being as tall as me. I thought it was the coolest thing ever that you'd get a prize that was as tall as you and big as you. . . . Over the years I've won a few more trophies, but that trophy was awfully memorable."[2]

Is it any surprise that Tiger, an only child, had no problem recalling an early childhood memory in which he was already dominating his competition? That trophy was "awfully memorable" precisely because Tiger is a driver, so he is apt to recall memories of achievement as a child. And achieve he did, for his list of wins—both here in the United States and abroad, as well as the firsts that he's accomplished in the sport of golf—read as if he created the game!

But while our society celebrates drivers' accomplishments, making them the subjects of inspirational movies and grocery-aisle-magazine cover articles, there are certainly dangers of being a driver to the detriment of your health and your relationships. Today, almost 40 percent of American workers are working more than 50 hours each week.[3] Though the driver's lifestyle has many positive aspects, it can take over your life and become unhealthy.

Pushed farther and farther, drivers can become controllers.

A controller believes, *I only count in life when I exercise power*

A controller believes, *I only count in life when I exercise power over those around me.* *over those around me.* The strength of the controller is that he or she often sees what needs to be done, so that person can be good at directing people—provided that directing is done in a healthy, non-bossy manner. But the controllers' slippery slope into dysfunction is that of interacting in unhealthy ways with those around them.

Here's what I mean. I was speaking at a church one Sunday and during the break between the first and second services all the pastors gathered in the senior pastor's office to pray. As one of the associate pastors entered the room, the senior pastor walked over to him, squared off in his face, and began screaming at him. He was an inch away, yelling in no uncertain terms that he wanted the chairs in the sanctuary twenty inches apart, not eighteen! But the worst part was that Reverend Hothead then stopped screaming, looked at his watch, and, in one of the most surreal transitions I've seen, said, "Let's pray." What does that incident say about that guy's need for control? I'd hate to be around him if I mistakenly printed the bulletin insert on plain yellow paper instead of goldenrod.

Controllers often take life way too seriously. Every decision becomes a matter of black and white, right and wrong—based on the controller's criteria, of course. The controller strives toward perfection and holds that template for everyone else to live up to. I don't know about you, but my experience shows that striving for 100 percent perfection for yourself or anybody else is a formula that guarantees a 100 percent chance of failure. That extreme way of viewing life simply doesn't work when applied to real situations and real people.

So am I saying that no one should be in charge? Certainly not. We need people willing and able to take the reins of leadership. Believe me, if there's a 13-car pileup along Interstate 10 here in Tucson, I want someone to come screaming in with sirens blaring and take control of the situation! But that pastor's blowup is a classic example of an unhealthy controller—someone who sacrifices reasonable, healthy interaction with fellow human beings for two inches between chairs. Not a great trade in my book. And I bet the associate pastor he was screaming at felt the same way.

I wish I could say that incident was an isolated example, but unfortunately controllers are everywhere, somehow spurred on by the misguided notion that leadership is best exercised at high decibels with flying spittle. Controlling others can also be deceptively subtle, such as when a husband won't "let" his wife drive the new car, which incidentally doesn't make him a "driver." It makes him a controller. When controllers shift from controlling a situation to controlling people, when leadership turns to an exercise of power, then "Houston, we have a problem." I think it's not only a problem; it's downright wrong.

I guess controlling would be a great quality to have if you want to overthrow a small, third-world country by military coup and become a dictator.

Just don't say I didn't warn you about the consequences.

A Little Give and Take . . .

I can't think of a better contemporary example of the lifestyle of a giver than the late Mother Teresa, who gave virtually her entire life to selflessly serving the poor, the sick, and the dying of Calcutta, India.

What were her childhood memories?

Interestingly, Mother Teresa was very hesitant to talk about her childhood. "Mine was a happy family," she said. "I had one brother and one sister, but I do not like to talk about it. It is not important now. The important thing is to follow God's way, the way he leads us to do something beautiful for him."[4]

But though she didn't care to focus on her family, it is clear that her mother's efforts to reach out to the poor made an impact on her. As an adult, Mother Teresa recalled her mother feeding and providing clothes to strangers, whom she thought at the time were her relatives. Specifically, her childhood memories included helping her mother care for an alcoholic woman covered in sores and visiting a dying mother of six children.[5] Is it any surprise that childhood memories of givers are going to likely include—hold your breath—experiences that emphasize the importance of giving?

I once heard the story about a little boy who stood out in his classroom because of his physical differences. Consequently, his mother was worried that on Valentine's Day no one would give him a Valentine card . . . even though he had poured himself into making cards for everyone else in the class. When he came home, however, he said, "Look, Mommy, I gave away all of my Valentine cards!" The farthest thing from that boy's mind was what he got. Instead, what mattered to his private logic was what he gave.

75

> A giver believes, *I only count in life when I'm contributing to others' well-being.*

A giver believes, *I only count in life when I'm contributing to others' well-being.* Givers are the kind of people that you might find later in life in the helping professions as doctors, nurses, counselors, and social workers. They don't have to be told that it is more blessed to give than receive because they already feel that truth intrinsically and live it out in their day-to-day decisions.

That's not the case with everyone, of course. Some are takers. A taker believes, *I only count in life when I'm receiving from others.*

My wife, Sande, has an early childhood memory of walking to the store with her cousin to buy candy. They were both given a quarter by Sande's parents, but the boy pocketed his own quarter and smooth-talked her into paying for both of them. Sande, who would give the proverbial shirt off her back, is still all too happy to give whatever she can to others. Those at the opposite end of the spectrum, however—those with the taker lifestyle, like that young boy Sande walked to the store with—feel that they are playing their role in life only when they are on the receiving end from others.

Granted, there's strength in knowing what you need in life, but the taker's lifestyle can become a form of power that he or she exercises. Typical takers' childhood memories might involve how they were able to get others to do something they were supposed to do themselves. If the taker lifestyle fits your personality, you probably didn't see manipulating others as a bad thing—you probably felt it was a victory.

One young woman remembered getting her little sister to do her job of picking up the living room while she was out riding her bike. Because that young woman was a taker, her feeling was one of satisfaction. She felt on top of the world because she got someone else to do what she was supposed to do. And she got away with it too!

A taker believes, *I only count in life when I'm receiving from others.*

Whether you're a giver or a taker, remember not to let your lifestyle lead you to relate to people in unhealthy ways. I'd encourage you takers to develop an awareness of those around you and their needs. If you don't, you're in danger of becoming controllers. So when your first instinct is to think, *Hey, what can I get out of this?* change your internal questions to *What does the other person need? How can I encourage him or make her comfortable?* Even if you have to go out of your own way to do so, it'll help you shift from taking to giving.

My caution to you givers is that you also develop an awareness to keep controllers or takers from walking all over you. When someone asks you to jump, think before you respond, "Okay. How high?" For instance, don't do all the work for the controller on the committee. Decide ahead of time what tasks you would like to do and are capable of doing with your current schedule, then set boundaries. No is not a dirty word. Givers need to learn to use it for their own sanity and health's sake.

If you don't set those boundaries, watch out! Because any giver lifestyle—when pushed to the extreme—might easily become a pleaser or a martyr.

When Others Matter Too Much

Have you ever worried what someone thought about you? Sometimes what people think about us matters too much. Remember that woman whose childhood memory was of her parents correcting how she folded the laundry? Well, if I were making a guess, I'd say that woman probably had at least some of the *pleaser* lifestyle at work within her.

> A pleaser believes,
> *I only count when I'm*
> *making others happy.*

A pleaser believes, *I only count when I'm making others happy.* The kind of memories that a pleaser is likely to have are those of trying to impress her parents but never quite being able to measure up. Does that sound like your childhood memories, your private logic, and your lifestyle? If it does, you may quite likely still be living up to others' expectations of you—whether your cooking is good enough for your mother-in-law, whether you're always available to watch your neighbor's kids, or whether you should be the one to sign up again to do weekend overtime at work. It's certainly a wonderful thing to make others happy, but when your very worth hinges on it, something is wrong. Start living to please others and you inevitably live an instable life, blown back and forth by the winds of expectation.

In general, pleasers tend to be women. Why is that? Probably because socially men are seen as weak if they are pleasers, whereas in our culture women are praised if they are doing what others would like them to. Sadly, often women pleasers and controlling men end up together in relationships. At first the match feels like a good one—both play their given roles, which appear on the surface to dovetail together well. The man likes to control and the woman likes to please. But after a while,

77

the woman can lose patience with being walked over by the man and bring the relationship to a head. That means if you're a pleaser, beware! (For more on the pleaser lifestyle, see my book titled *Pleasers*.)

At the extreme end of the pleaser lifestyle is the lifestyle of a martyr, who is craving attention. A martyr believes, *I only count when I give myself up "nobly" for a cause.* That cause might be the family or it might be getting the husband to change his ways, but whatever it is, the martyr throws herself wholly into that cause to receive attention from those around her. "Oh, you poor thing!" the martyr's enabling neighbors say. "You organized the entire get-together and all the food yourself, and your husband didn't help at all?" The martyr's private logic is like that of the child who wants attention so badly he'll even settle for negative attention. The martyr's lifestyle may be an unhealthy way of getting attention, but it's still attention nevertheless. So as long as it feels good, she keeps doing it.

> A martyr believes, *I only count when I give myself up "nobly" for a cause.*

Remember that taker's memory in which the woman as a young girl was able to smooth-talk her younger sibling into cleaning the living room? A martyr's childhood memory might be formed on the receiving end of that experience, giving in to her older sister and cleaning that living room, thinking all along what a wonderful sister she is for doing the work so her sister can ride her bike. Does that little martyr feel that the situation is unfair? Not at all. In fact, she sees it as an opportunity to give beyond what she should reasonably be giving.

If you see traces of the pleaser or martyr lifestyle in yourself, remember that while your thoughts and concerns for others and doing their work are admirable, the danger you face is in letting everyone walk all over you or in selling yourself short for negative attention. Resist that "martyr sigh" that punctuates all you do. Hold on to your care and concern for others, but be vigilant in learning to set appropriate boundaries, saying no when your private logic pulls you to say, "Oh, sure, I'll do that for you!"

Charming, Aren't They?

Just in case you haven't figured it out by now, my lifestyle is that of a *charmer.* I've charmed my way into traveling first class on an airplane. I've charmed my way to free tickets for my family to get into Disney World's Epcot Center. My litmus test of whether I'm doing well in a television interview is whether or not I'm able to charm the camera crew into laughing during the filming. I know they've seen Robin Williams before and they've heard Bill Cosby. *So who is the chubby little psychologist from Tucson?* they wonder. Nobody cares. But there's the challenge I see before me: If I can get that crew to laugh, then it's made my day, according to my lifestyle.

During one interview at Chicago's WGN-TV we were talking about my book *Sheet Music*, a very straightforward look at marital sexual intimacy. When we started the interview, the camera crew was reading newspapers. But after a while, that crew, the support staff, and the interns were all gathered right behind the cameras forming a semicircle around our show. The female host was laughing so hard she couldn't get a word out. She actually held up her notes in front of her face on camera because she couldn't stop laughing and blushing!

As the fun-loving baby of my family, that's the kind of reaction I seek from people. That's the kind of attention a charmer loves!

Remember my childhood memory of gravitating to the spotlight during the Williamsville Billies basketball game? Or Jay Leno's memory of wanting to slide down the banister into the center of his parents' bridge game? Those are the kinds of memories that a charmer is likely to have—memories of fun and games, memories that center around birthday parties, holidays, and gifts that he or she received. A charmer believes, *I only count when I'm the center of attention.*

A charmer believes,
*I only count when I'm
the center of attention.*

If you, like me, are a charmer, you have all sorts of positive aspects to your personality. You have inherent social skills. You're probably quite comfortable in front of a group. If there's a presentation to be done at work or a class to be taught at your place of worship, then you're a great candidate to do it. But there's a flip side to your strengths—one I know all too well. You might become so focused on charming others to get your own way, wiggling your way into the center of attention, that you begin to neglect those around you.

My encouragement for you is to use the wonderful skills you've been given. After all, not everyone is as comfortable as you are in social situations. At the same time, don't believe for a moment that the world revolves around you—or that it should. It simply doesn't. But if you are able to apply the strengths of your charmer lifestyle with humility, you can make the world a much brighter place for others simply by being you!

Are You in the Stands or on the Field?

When I was an assistant dean of students at the University of Arizona, part of my job was helping students get involved in the activities there. And, boy, there were a bunch to choose from! Today, if you'd like to meet other budding physicians, lawyers, or automotive engineers, there are groups for precisely that purpose. Interested in practicing your German? or playing sand volleyball? How about aerial robotics? Surfing club—in Arizona! Women's ice hockey? The percussion club? Rubik's Cube organization for those who like puzzles? Anyone for dodgeball?

It's all there if you're a student wanting to get involved.

While I was working there at the University of Arizona I got to know a woman who played in the band. That's a great activity to participate in, but unfortunately she didn't show her face much beyond that. For whatever reason, she kept herself separate from other students. She never entered the student union building, and as far as I know, she is still living a solitary life to this day.

When a person is sharing an early childhood memory with me about, say, performing an impromptu play in the living room for the adults or playing a game of street football with the neighborhood kids, I pay attention to who the play's "artistic director" was and who the team captain or quarterback was. That perspective in your memory of either standing back and observing or of participating in the action can be a key indicator to how you live your life today.

Some people are observers at heart, sitting on the sidelines and watching life go by. Others are participants, getting involved in the action and perhaps even leading it. As an observer, you might be more able than others to see the big picture, but you may also sit back and not get involved when you should. Participants, on the other hand, love to get involved and can make great leaders, but they also can lose sight of the proverbial forest for the trees.

Whichever one you are, don't let the weaknesses of your lifestyle outweigh the strengths. Observers, keep assessing your environment with your keen eye, but also go out of your way to get involved and relate to those around you. Participants, keep right on digging in with gusto, but you might want to consciously step back every now and then to make sure that you're not losing perspective. Also, make sure that others—those observers—are participating with you, and that you're heading in the right direction.

You *Do* Count in Life. Period.

We've only begun to cover the infinite number of lifestyles possible. There are people who find their worth in rationalizing their every action. There are people who see themselves as bad, no matter what they do. Then, of course, there are the goody-goodies, people whose

Lifestyle Strengths and Weaknesses

	STRENGTH	WEAKNESS
Driver	Gets things done	Can drive to the neglect of relationships
Controller	Takes control of situations needing firm leadership	Often domineers people
Pleaser	Considers others' needs	Can please others to the neglect of his or her own needs
Martyr	Considers others' needs	Leverages others' needs to get attention
Giver	Considers others' needs	Sometimes overlooks his or her own needs
Taker	Knows what he or she wants	Often struggles with selfishness
Charmer	Enjoys being the life of the party	Sometimes craves attention to the neglect of others
Observer	Sees the big picture	Can be tempted to sit out
Participant	Likes getting involved	Could get involved in too many activities, unable to say no

private logic says they must always be seen by others in a good light. And there are those of us whose lifestyle says it's better to be seen and not heard. There are arguably thousands of lifestyle patterns for the way people live out the way they see themselves in relation to others and to the world around them, and because all of us are complex individuals, none of us can be pegged into simply one lifestyle. You are a blend of lifestyles, whether a driving giver, a charming controller, or a goody-goody martyr content to sit on the sidelines and observe. But whatever your particular blend of lifestyles, there's a danger common to them all: that of falling into the rut of your lifestyle's weakness until it takes over you, rather than you taking charge over it.

Have you ever heard of the game Two Truths & One Lie? Each person in the group thinks of two pieces of trivia that are true about herself and one that is false. Then, one by one, each person takes turns sharing their three "facts," and the group tries to guess which ones are true and which one is false. It's a simple way to learn fun tidbits about each other, even those friends you know well!

I bring that up because while some people claim to not be so good at concocting stories—at lying—I'd disagree. You're an excellent storyteller. In fact, there's a tale you tell so well that you have yourself believing it! That tale is that you matter in life only when you're living according to your lifestyle. It's one of the most commonly believed lies ever created by humanity—that you matter only when you give to others beyond your capacity, or only when you perform flawlessly, or only when you control others or they control you.

It's easy to believe the lies, to stagger into the bathroom in the morning and stare disappointedly into the mirror at the wrinkles under your eyes, your blemished skin, or your graying hair, not to mention all the flaws you know are inside. You may not see yourself in your best light, but I guarantee you this—Almighty God does. And after seeing so many people from all walks of life make the changes they needed to after examining their private logic and unique lifestyle, I know you can make those changes too! You don't only matter when you're following the rigid rules of your lifestyle.

You matter simply because you are uniquely you!

CHAPTER 6

Be Your Own Shrink

Take a stroll down memory lane

Have you ever walked into a room to get something, then stood there perplexed, having completely forgotten what you went there for? What do you do when that happens? You might stand there for a moment, trying to recall why you're there. *Boy, I know I came here for something. . . .* You might look around for clues. *Was it the laundry? To make a phone call?* You might close your eyes as you think back a minute, trying to remember your errand. *Now, let's see. I was going through my day. . . .* But, ultimately, if you simply can't remember what you went there for no matter how hard you try, what do you do?

You go back into the room you came from.

Oftentimes when we return to the place we just came from, it immediately jogs our memory. A wonderfully mysterious process of association happens when we travel back physically or mentally to places we left only a few moments ago—or, as you'll see in this chapter, decades ago. Our brain picks up the connections again and is able to recall things more easily by association. You might return to your living room, see the light falling on your desk, and remember, *Oh, yeah! I was standing here looking out the window when I saw my neighbor poking around under the hood of his car, which reminded me that I needed a pencil from the kitchen to write myself a note to change our car's oil.*

You're probably familiar with that kind of mental slip.

I've certainly forgotten my share of events. I was once picking up burgers for the family when the business phone there at the burger joint rang and the guy behind the counter answered it.

"It there a Leman here?" he called out into the restaurant.

That's odd, I thought as I raised my hand and walked over to take the phone from him. *Who knows I'm here?*

"Dad!" said the voice over the line.

"Krissy?!" I said, taken aback.

"Dad!" she repeated, cutting me off. "Do you know where you're supposed to be?"

"I'm picking up burgers for the family. Krissy, let's talk about this when I—"

"No, Dad!" she said, interrupting me again. "You're supposed to be speaking at the Holiday Inn—right now! It's a standing-room-only crowd!"

I'd remembered to brush my teeth that morning and zip my fly. I'd remembered the directions to reach the burger joint, and I'd even remembered each family member's lunch order. Yet I stood there in my baseball cap, Arizona Wildcats T-shirt, and shorts, having completely forgotten one of the most important events of the day—my scheduled speaking engagement at the local Rotary Club luncheon. Why couldn't I remember that?! The man behind the counter handed me my burgers, but by then I'd lost my appetite.

As we've talked about your childhood memories over the past few chapters, perhaps you've been thinking, *Dr. Leman, this is all very nice information—thanks for sharing. But it doesn't do me any good. I can't remember a thing from my childhood.*

Don't worry. I talk with people all the time who can't remember their childhood memories at first. Frankly, who can blame them? If I can't keep my speaking engagement in my noggin for a few hours, who's to fault you for not being able to remember skinning a knee two or three decades ago? Even if your memory is razor sharp and nothing slips by you, recalling childhood memories still involves retrieving fleeting sights and sounds tucked away in some dusty corner of your mental archives. And many of those memories were stored before you even knew how to ride a bike. Accessing forgotten childhood memories is a bit like hacking through an overgrown trail. The trail is there, but it may take a bit of work to follow it and reach your destination.

Thankfully, recalling your childhood memories isn't as difficult as you might think. Consider the long-forgotten memories that rush back unexpectedly when you smell a pine tree on the breeze. Instantly that aroma brings back memories of camping with your family during the summer. Or you hear a song that you haven't heard in years and all sorts of memories surface from when you listened to that song over and over. How many times have you said to yourself, I haven't thought about that for years?

87

Your memories aren't always immediately accessible, but they are there.

Row, Row, Row Your Boat, Gently down the Stream

As you begin recalling your childhood memories, you'll find that while at first your mind may feel completely blank, as you allow yourself time and space to follow traces of your memories, you'll almost certainly begin to uncover a memory or two, which usually then leads you to more. It's like following a trickle down a mountain. The farther you follow it, the more it grows—first into a little creek, then a stream, then a river.

That's precisely the way it is when you set aside time to revisit your memories. If you give yourself time in a quiet place to think back on your childhood, I'll bet that you'll be able to recall many of your most vivid memories. It may help to set aside time to journal or talk with a trusted friend about your memories. Find a place where you feel comfortable—outside, inside, or wherever you please—and perhaps grab a cup of coffee or tea if that will help you relax. You might even try listening to music from the time of your childhood to help you think back. You may notice how much easier it is to remember events in your life when you are able to create a space to quiet your busy mind and keep life's distractions from pressing in.

Track Your Childhood Memories

Describe your memory in 2–4 sentences.	
What were your feelings attached to the memory?	
What was the most vivid part of your memory?	
How old were you?	
Now you be the shrink. Write down what you think this memory reveals about who you are.	

Whether you're by yourself or talking with a friend, allow your mind to wander from memory to memory. Your memories may start out vague—which is normal—but as you allow yourself to travel down the stream of your memories, you will probably find yourself coming across more and more vivid memories, like that mountain creek joining streams, then rivers.

As you try this exercise, I've provided you with some specific entry points to think about, journal in response to, or discuss with a friend to help get you started along the road to uncovering your private logic and lifestyle. To make things even easier for those of you with organized temperaments, I've put together a chart to help you track your early childhood memories.

What sort of memories are you likely to discover and track? Here are a few of the most common ones, to give you a start.

89

School

For many people—especially firstborns and only children—school is associated with early childhood memories because school provides the first major proving ground for children to receive attention from their parents and other adults. Here are some prompts related to school:

- How did you get to school—by walking, riding a bus, being driven in a carpool, or being driven by a parent or other caretaker? What do you remember about those times?
- Did you like school? Why or why not?
- Can you recall the names of any of your friends? What do you remember about them?
- What happened at recess that you liked or didn't like?
- Do you remember receiving any awards or winning any competitions at school? Do you remember losing any competitions or failing in school? How did you feel?
- Who were your favorite and least favorite teachers? Why?
- Did you ever visit the principal's office? Why were you there?

Summer vacations

What you did during family summers or vacations will often provide springboards to other memories.

• What specifically did your family do during summers or vacations?
• Did you take any trips? Where did you go, and what makes you remember that trip?
• Did you visit any relatives or have them over to your home? What was this interaction like?
• What were holidays like at your home, including Christmases and Thanksgivings?

House(s) you lived in

Picture the house(s) you grew up in and imagine yourself walking through the rooms, in the yard, and through the neighborhood. If appropriate, visit the neighborhood in person and even see if you can walk through the house itself for "old time's sake" to allow childhood memories to surface.

• What specific memories surface about your parent(s), siblings?
• What feelings do you have associated with each specific room of the house? What events caused those feelings?
• Do you remember any fights between your parents? Did either of your parents struggle with alcohol or drug addiction?

Mind the Details . . .

Sometimes when people share their childhood memories with me, they'll say something such as "I remember as a little kid going to the beach a lot," or "I sure had a sad childhood."

I don't doubt that you practically lived in your swimsuit with sand always between your toes during those summer months of growing up. Or that you feel deep loss wash over you as you think back to your childhood. But if what comes to mind as you recall your childhood memories is not a particular event, unfortunately it doesn't give us the specific details we need to learn about your private logic and unique lifestyle.

Mother Teresa, who was very hesitant to talk about her childhood because she felt it detracted from helping others follow God's path, said, "I remember my mother, my father and the rest of us praying together each evening. . . . It is God's greatest gift to the family. It maintains family unity. The family that does not pray together does not stay together."[1] But notice that while Mother Teresa's memory is true to her experience and undoubtedly powerful, it is not a specific memory, but is instead a generalization of her memories. She remembered praying in general, not a specific experience of praying together that made a particular impact.

The fact that trips to the beach were a regular part of family life, that you have an overarching feeling of sadness regarding your childhood, or that you remember praying together as a family are important recollections. But before you can apply the principles in this book to your life, you need a specific memory to work with. Otherwise you may be generalizing about a compilation of memories, expounding on stories that your family has told you over the years, or imagining experiences to accompany images you've seen in a photo album or on home videos.

If you're thinking, *But what I remember about my childhood is that my family was at the beach all the time,* let me ask you this: Do any incidents in particular stand out over the course of your family's time at the beach? Do you have feelings that accompany those memories? What specific events made your childhood sad or happy?

These are important points to distinguish because when you're thinking back to assess your memories, you need to mind the details.

Note what words you use.
Earlier I pointed out that firstborns' and only children's memories tend to have more detail than people in other birth orders. But even if you

> Pay attention to the specifics in your memories, because the details that you remember, you remember for a reason.

aren't the firstborn son or daughter in your family, pay attention to the specifics in your memories, because the details that you remember, you remember for a reason.

Some time ago I spoke at a weekend marriage conference. To illustrate how birth order plays into who we marry and how we interact in our relationships, I asked for one couple to stand and tell me about themselves. Out of six hundred people in the audience, one woman jumped to her feet as if she had been waiting all weekend for this chance. Her husband, on the other hand, sat there blinking in shock, about as willing to join in as if his wife had volunteered the two of them to do an impromptu song-and-dance routine.

"Billy," I said to him after asking his name, "I can see you haven't consented to this. Your wife's on her feet and 598 people are looking at you to see what you're going to do. If you want to opt out and make a fool of yourself, you're welcome to do that. But I think that you'll probably have to pay the consequences later with your wife."

Everyone laughed, and since I had broken the ice for Billy, he agreed.

As part of the exercise, I wanted them to share some of their childhood memories dealing with their parents. So I turned to the wife and said, "Start with a description of your dad."

"My dad is very laid-back," she began. "Unfortunately he let the women in his life run over him. He was very cooperative—often to a fault. I remember . . ." As she went on to describe her father, I listened not only to her childhood account of the influence he had had in her life but also to what she was telling us about herself by the words she chose to describe her memories. I picked up on the fact that she frequently used the word very as she described her family. She was giving us all a clue about how she saw life—in very black-and-white terms, which is a trait especially common to only children.

As you explore your own childhood memories, pay attention to the words you use to describe them. If you are sharing your childhood memories with a friend or spouse, ask that person to pay attention to your words, because they often provide a clue to your private logic. If you're journaling, using the Track Your Childhood Memories chart on page 88, review what you've written to see if there are any words that you repeated or that you felt strongly about as you wrote them. Perhaps you wrote, "When my mother told me to go to the pool snack bar and ask the person behind the counter for a glass of water, I wanted her to do it. I really wanted my mother to go get it for me." Notice the repetition of the word wanted and the concept of someone else doing for you what you could do yourself. That might correspond to your desire for others to do things for you, which could indicate a lifestyle today of shying away from doing things yourself and passing up wonderful opportunities.

Remember, everyone's private logic is different, so each person is going to emphasize different aspects of even similar memories and, consequently, use different words in their descriptions. That's why others—especially siblings—can have opposite feelings and recollections of the exact same event.

Consider my memory of being locked out on the front porch when I was three years old. If someone else had precisely the same experience, she might emphasize the fear of being separated from family by using such words as apart or separated when describing that memory. That would lead me to believe that togetherness and relationships probably matter immensely to that person. While I had some of those feelings during my own experience, if I was telling you the story of that memory, you'd hear me talking about "locked doors" and "being outside, looking in." The fact that those are the words I use tells you a lot about the lens through which I see that experience and life in

93

general. To me that memory is about feeling locked out and banging on closed doors in my life. Those were the issues that mattered to me as a child then, and those are issues that still matter to me now.

So ask yourself these questions:

- What words am I using as I tell the stories of my memories? Why am I choosing *those* words?
- Are there any words that I repeat as I describe my memories? Why?
- As I write down my memory or talk about it with a friend, do I feel strongly about any of the words I use? In other words, do certain parts just *have* to be said or the story feels incomplete?

94

Share your feelings.

Perhaps you've noticed something about my memories that I've shared with you—all of them had a feeling of mine attached. In my memory of botching the Williamsville Billies cheer, there was the elation at making people laugh. In my memory of being on the front porch of our house, there was the frustration of being locked on the outside, unable to get in. And in my memory of smoking the Viceroy cigarette, there was my pride for joining the rebellious neighborhood trouble-maker, Eddy.

Did you notice the feelings expressed in others' memories, too? Fred Rogers feared making mistakes when he played the electric organ on his front porch in his neighborhood, and Steven Spielberg feared driving into the night to watch meteors. In fact, if you tell me a child-hood memory and I ask, "Can you attach a feeling to that memory?" and you can't, then most likely it isn't a memory of yours.

Stumped? Here's what I mean. If you can't remember a feeling associated with your memory, it's likely that "memory" is actually a story you were told at some point in time or simply a story that your mind concocted after looking at, say, a photo album or home-video clip. This isn't to say that what you remember about that incident didn't actually happen or that it doesn't reveal things about yourself. It might.

But because your childhood memories are stored in your long-term memory by your emotions and because those emotions reveal how you interpreted those experiences—in other words, your private logic—it's important to focus on your feelings associated with your memories.

Otherwise, you may be recalling something as simple and two-dimensional as a photo.

So ask yourself these questions:

- What feelings are associated with each of my memories?
- As I write down my memories or tell them to a friend, what feelings return as I tell the stories?

95

Photographic Memory or Remembering Photographs?

Church was a tad boring for me at age three, as I imagine it is for most three-year-olds. At that age we're all much more interested in drawing bug-eyed stick figures on the church bulletin and seeing how far we can swing our legs back to kick the underside of the church pews. I'm not sure how I managed to sit through sermons on sanctification, justification, and all the rest of the "ifications," but my mother sure remembered—apparently I *didn't* sit. I went off exploring. Right in the middle of the service!

When I was older, she told me the story of how I'd slip away from her in church and wriggle under the pews like a greased pig escaping under a fence. If that weren't enough, because women would take off their shoes to get more comfortable during the sermon, I would take one woman's shoes and switch them with another's. I would go down five or six rows like that, switching shoes willy-nilly, my three-year-old idea of a church potluck.

When I first heard that story, I laughed like crazy—that certainly was me! Because that story is so consistent with the kinds of things I did at that age and because I've now heard that story told time and time again, I could easily fool myself and begin believing that that story is part of my memory. But since I don't remember that childhood story—because I don't have a feeling attached to it—it's not an early childhood memory of mine.

I bring this up because as you take time to think back, you need to assess whether your memory truly is your memory and not the prompting of someone else. Sometimes we think we remember an event when really we're just retelling a story that's been told to us as we grew up, or imagining ourselves into an event that we've seen in a photo album or on a home movie.

How can you tell the difference?

Again, if you don't have a feeling associated with it, it's probably not an early childhood memory of yours. Own it as one of your memories, and you'll begin fooling yourself.

Take the famous twentieth-century artist Picasso, who began to believe things about himself that were simply being reflected back to him by others regarding his childhood:

> I have never done children's drawings. Never. Even when I was very small. I remember one of my first drawings. I was perhaps six, or even less [i.e., 1887]. In my father's house there was a statue of Hercules with his club in the corridor, and I drew Hercules. But it wasn't a child's drawing. It was a real drawing, representing Hercules with his club.[2]

One biography of Picasso's said about that memory, "Wishful thinking played him false. Picasso had forgotten that the drawing in question is dated November 1890—that is to say, three years later than he thought. The execution and conception are no more or less mature than one would expect of a gifted nine-year-old."[3]

Is it possible that the stories told to Picasso about his artistic genius went to his head, causing him to "remember" his childhood art as better than it was? Yes, I think so, because sometimes the stories we're told by those around us cause us to believe them to be our own, when in fact they're only stories placed there by others. But using the test of whether or not you have a feeling attached to your memory will help you assess whether it's truly a memory of yours or not.

What Do You Remember before Age Eight?

If you've ever visited the county fair you've probably seen those signs near the amusement-park rides that show some little loony character holding his hand out and a message that reads, "You must be at least this tall to ride the rides." Well, in order for you to assess your childhood memories, I'm holding up a sign—loony character that I am—that reads, "Your childhood memories must be under this age for us to assess them."

Psychologists may disagree on how much of each person's personality is formed by nature and how much is formed by nurture. We may disagree on precisely how a mother or father influences the life of a child. But while we may not agree on everything, if there's one thing we psychologists do agree on, it's that a person's personality is generally formed in the first five to six years of life.

> Your personality is generally formed in the first five to six years of your life.

Most children's earliest childhood memories occur around three years old, perhaps because by age three many children begin entering a wider social network—either through preschool, play groups, or simply by interacting with other neighborhood children on a more regular basis—so they're exposed to more stimulating interaction with others. But their interaction with people from birth to age two consists mainly of Dad and Mom, and Grandma and Grandpa.

Interestingly enough, you're more likely to recall memories from periods in your life other than your early childhood. One Duke psychologist noted that your memories between the ages of 10 and 30 stand out more than others throughout your life. Why? The good doctor hypothesized that it could be simply because our brains are at their sharpest during that time, that we are experiencing a lot of "firsts" and emotionally charged events during that period, or that we're still trying to navigate our way toward and into adulthood, so we're more apt to recall that process of discovery.[4]

But while you can learn a thing or two about yourself from your teenage memories or your memories from yesterday afternoon, those memories don't carry nearly the same significance when it comes to assessing your foundational private logic. If you remember something between the time you were born and eight years of age, it's going to be significant, an experience that your psyche stored for a reason. It's going to be a memory that makes some sense of your place in the world, prompted, in other words, by your private logic and unique lifestyle.

You'll notice that I pointed out that psychologists agree that a person's personality is formed from birth to about age six, yet I'm suggesting you consider memories up to age eight. Because psychology is not an exact science and people mature at different rates (I'm living proof of that latter point), you can't expect that the day you turn seven your memories no longer provide valuable information about your private logic. The lines are much more blurred. You could no more pin down precisely when someone is going to start and end puberty than you could pin down at what age childhood memories are no longer triggered by your private logic. I want you to consider your memories up to age eight because personality generally forms in the first five to six years of life, and I've just stretched the line a couple years to allow for variances among different people.

Out of the Minds of Babes

There are those of us who can't seem to recall any memories earlier than high school. Then there are those who seem to remember so far back you wonder how they do it.

Dr. James Dobson, founder of Focus on the Family, once told me his earliest memory—and when it happened he must have been about nine months old! As he related it, he was on a porch and sunlight was streaming through the window. He remembers feeling comfort from being held, and though he doesn't remember who was feeding him, he remembers he was being fed Pablum formula.

I'm certainly not going to argue with the only child! If anybody can recall a memory at nine months old, it would be Jim Dobson. Notice that the feeling he has attached to the memory is one of warmth and security. He was being loved and held, and if there's one man who has done that for others through the decades, it's Jim Dobson through the work he's done at Focus on the Family. Millions of people whose lives have been helped by Jim love and respect him.

Most people begin remembering things around age three, so it's very rare to have a childhood memory earlier than age two—but there are people who do. I call these very early memories "crib memories," and again they manifest a child's interpretation of the environment in which he or she lives. Interestingly enough, over the past three decades, I've discovered something unique about those with crib memories: For whatever reason, those who have crib memories tend to be highly creative people.

Director Steven Spielberg also has a crib memory of entering a Cincinnati synagogue for services with Hasidic elders. "I wasn't a religious kid," he recalled, "although I was [later] Bar Mitzvahed in a real Orthodox synagogue. The old men were handing me little crackers. My parents said later I must have been about six months old!"[5] He doesn't say whether there's a feeling attached to the memory, so I can't be sure if it's truly a memory of his and not a story that was passed down to him. But if we accept Spielberg's memory as his own, then it's further evidence that crib memories are indicative of highly creative people. After all, if a list were made of those living today who could be said to be creative, Steven Spielberg would certainly make it on there somewhere!

99

Seek a Grouping of Memories

As you evaluate your childhood memories, it's easy to get caught up in trying to remember back as far as possible, somehow buying into the belief that the earlier the memory, the more "pure" and, therefore, accurate the memory is. Some people who are charting their early childhood memories ask themselves, *Can I remember back to age five? age four? before age three?*

There's probably a reason why you remember your very earliest memory, but don't forget that your personality and private logic are still being formed throughout your early years. Just because you remember an event in your life at age two and a half doesn't make it more telling than the trio of memories you can recall from when you were five. As revealing as crib memories can be, what is even more important in exploring your early memories are the patterns that emerge among the collection of your memories.

In other words, I would place more weight on a group of three of your childhood memories than on one earliest memory. You will get a more accurate picture of your private logic by assembling a composite group of memories from your early years in order to better understand your life's themes.

If There's Trauma in Your Past . . .

I once counseled a man who was having issues with his temper. When I asked him about his early childhood memories to learn more about his private logic and lifestyle, he simply replied, "I don't have any childhood memories."

As I mentioned, it's fairly common for people to not initially remember their childhood memories very clearly, so I tried prompting him by asking him about the house he grew up in, the schools he attended, interactions with childhood friends, etc. But after a few minutes it became clear that he really couldn't go back before his sixteenth birthday.

So I asked him, "Did anything happen to you when you were sixteen?"

"My father shot himself," he said very matter-of-factly. "Then my younger sister came upon his body and killed herself with the same gun."

No wonder he didn't have any childhood memories. That experience in his midteens had caused an iron curtain to be pulled over the early years of that man's life, and he had never looked back. Though as an adult he was a successful businessman, he paid for it in his relationships by putting up off-limits signs because of the debilitating pain he felt inside.

Many of you reading those words have also faced severe trauma in your past. It may be experiences of neglect, abandonment, rape, or other horrific emotional, physical, verbal, or sexual abuse. I first want to say that no one—no one!—ever deserved the treatment you experienced. My heart truly goes out to you. I wish I could rewind the years for you to the time before the trauma happened. I wish I could take away the pain.

If you know or suspect that you may have been through such trauma, you will need more than just this book to come to terms with those experiences and begin the process of healing. If you haven't already, I strongly advise you to talk in person with a counselor, therapist, or minister trained to help you work through traumatic experiences such as what you've been through. If this book serves no other purpose than to direct you to professional help, I will be grateful.

Most of Oprah's fans are aware of her own experience of being raped as a 9-year-old child by her 19-year-old cousin.[6] In order to encourage people to grow past their painful pasts, Oprah talked publicly about her own pain and struggles. "I understand that many people are victimized," she once said, "and some people certainly more horribly than I have been. But you have to be responsible for claiming your own victories, you really do. If you live in the past and allow the past to define who you are, then you never grow."[7]

This step is so important. I'll say it again: If you find yourself facing memories of abuse in your past that have not been dealt with and you picked up this book looking for direction, then you have found the direction you need—seek the help of a qualified professional to talk through the pain that is holding you back.

It's easy to put Oprah on a pedestal because of her celebrity status today. But think of her humble, impoverished roots and all the years she struggled with the fallout of her incest, poor self-image, drug abuse, weight gain, and getting pregnant as a young teenager.[8] But instead of staying stuck in the past, she became the host of one of the most popular television shows ever, where people are invited to talk about their own stories of overcoming crippling pain. So many people have sat on her couch—some of them with stories similar to yours. Clearly, Oprah is passionate about portraying people (like herself) with traumatic pasts who are living proof that, no matter what you've been through, you can make it!

Remember This . . .

If, after thinking back on your childhood and asking yourself the questions that I've included in this chapter, you still can't recall many childhood memories, don't worry. You can't force them. They'll come eventually, and when they do they'll come naturally, perhaps when you least expect them. When they do,

> No matter what you've been through, you can make it!

jot them down, including the feelings you have attached to them, however vague. As you begin to recall more and find your childhood memories revealing who you are—your personality, your strengths and weaknesses, your private logic, your unique lifestyle, and even clues to what you should be doing in life—remember one final, crucial point.

Memories are also tainted by lies.

That's right. Up to this point we've focused primarily on how your private logic and lifestyle in your childhood memories reveal who you are. But you're not immune to the lies that plague the way you see yourself in relation to others and the world around you. Chances are, your private logic is far from accurate, so as you get in touch with your childhood memories, bear in mind that the messages you receive from them—the private logic that you gather from those memories that form your lifestyle—not only reveal truths about who you are and how you are most likely to respond in a given situation.

They also reveal the lies that you tell yourself about yourself. And those lies—sneaky and underhanded as they are—can be most surprising! They will catch you off guard if you're not aware of them, and they'll wreak havoc in your life.

But when you learn to identify them, you gain the upper hand.

103

CHAPTER 7

The Truth about the Lies You Tell Yourself

Why you are more important than what you do

When I was a kid growing up in Williamsville, New York, my mother and I used to walk to Roger's Market, pulling one of those classic, red Radio Flyer wagons behind us. We'd do all of our shopping, pile our ten dollars' worth of groceries into that wagon (that bought about six bags back then!), and then pull it back home.

What stands out in my mind from that childhood memory, however, is the enormous hill we climbed to get to the grocery store. It towered over all of creation. Mount Everest was nothing compared to that hill between our house and the grocery store.

But if I were to drive you there today, I guarantee that you'd take one 360-degree look around at the horizon and say, "Uhh . . . where's the hill?"

"You're standing on it," I'd reply.

"This is the big hill?!" you'd say.

I'd nod. "Yeah, this is the place!"

Over the years I've returned there many times, and that "big hill" is probably two hundred yards long—barely a rise in the road. But to a little kid back then, it seemed to scrape the sky!

Isn't it amazing how selective your memory is and how prone it is to coloring your experiences with your interpretations? Perhaps you remember your childhood experiences through rose-tinted glasses, having stored away those cherished few moments of laughter together as a family instead of the frequent fights that happened at home. Others of you may remember the one or two conflicts that interrupted all the fun times—a very different focus based on your private logic. While the experiences chosen by your psyche for your memories are important, how you felt about the experiences and interpreted those memories matter ever so much more. And, unlike the facts of the events themselves, your feelings and interpretations are often skewed by lies.

> While the experiences chosen by your psyche for your memories are important, how you *felt* about the experiences and *interpreted* those memories matter ever so much more.

106

How Far Is It to the Tip of *Your* Nose?

Remember the story of Pinocchio? The little puppet wanted nothing more than to become a boy and feel his own heart beating inside his chest. He wanted arms and legs of flesh and bones rather than wood. But most importantly, he wanted a relationship with the one who created him.

He wanted to become a real boy.

But to do so, he had to learn the importance of being authentic and of telling the truth. Pinocchio got into all kinds of trouble along the way as the little wooden head's private logic was radically changed by his experiences.

There's a wonderful truth in this story, for without consciously knowing it, you may also be compromising the truth about yourself. Your lifestyle would have you believe the lie that you only matter when you're grinding yourself into the ground through your work, or that you only matter when you and your child are the center of attention at the neighborhood play group, or that you only matter when you're in control of the family budget and daily calendar. When you give in to this behavior, you become more like a marionette. Your strings are pulled by the lies you tell yourself!

This Pinocchio Syndrome, as I call it, happens when you reiterate those familiar lies about yourself and compromise who you really are. The more lies you tell yourself, the more your own nose starts growing and growing until—having fully bought into those lies—you begin to resemble the person you are at your core less and less. And just as Pinocchio wanted to become a real boy by telling the truth about himself, so you also need to acknowledge the lies you live through your lifestyle, through believing that you only matter by doing the things you do.

107

Do Memories = You Today?

I was speaking on the sanctity of marriage one Friday evening and I happened to mention the fact that people are counting on those of you who are married to stay married. Whether or not a marriage succeeds, I pointed out, matters to more people than simply you and your spouse. It matters to your children, if you have them. It matters to your extended family. And it matters to your friends and the larger community around you.

I'm not naïve. Believe me, after listening to many couples share their stories, I know the kinds of problems that exist in marriage. And I know that staying married can be one of the most difficult things to do when it feels as if you simply aren't making progress toward resolving your differences.

The next day, as I was signing books at the end of the morning session, a woman walked up to me and whispered in my ear, "I just want to tell you that what you shared last night and this morning really got my attention. You see, I had a moving van scheduled to be at my house next Friday as soon as my husband left for work. I was going to clean out the house and just head out of town." As I continued listening, I found that this woman had been living by the lie that she only mattered if she was pleasing her husband and keeping the peace at home. But as she did, her nose grew longer and longer, and their relationship continued to move farther and farther apart.

I never heard her childhood memories, but if I had, I'm guessing that they might have included being criticized for how she performed a chore around the house or not measuring up in some other way to her parents' expectations. It's quite likely that she grew up in a home where she didn't receive the love she needed, so like a moth to a flame, she was drawn to a man who was very critical of her, just as her own parents had probably been critical of her as a child. As a result, she grew into a pleaser.

108

"But you convinced me that my marriage is worth fighting for," she went on. "I'm not going to run from my differences with my husband any longer. I'm going to face them head-on and begin telling myself the truth about our relationship and about who I am."

Conversations such as that one make all my days spent jetting around the country, changing time zones as frequently as my underwear so I can talk with people about their relationships, worthwhile. I left that weekend so proud of that woman who was brave enough to begin telling herself the truth about the way she viewed her past, herself, and her marriage. She acknowledged her own lifestyle—her tendency to be a pleaser in her marriage—and made a difficult decision that would certainly require hard work, but that was an immensely positive step toward resolving the fights she and her husband were having.

As you look back at your childhood memories, do you see aspects of your lifestyle that you can identify as lies? Are you able to say, "Wow, I never saw it that way before, but you're right. That way I express my private logic is a lie. I certainly don't only matter when I'm doing that."

If you can, you're on your way to a much healthier you, because that objective awareness can literally change the course of your life.

Bono Fought the Consistency Factor

Bono, lead singer of what many would call the world's greatest band, U2, was once asked in an interview, "Do you have any idyllic childhood memories?"

"None at all," he replied. "The little pieces that I can put back together are, if not violent, then aggressive. I can remember my first day in school. I was introduced to this guy, James Mann, who, at age four, had the ambition of being a nuclear physicist, and one of the guys bit his ear. And I took that kid's head and banged it off an iron railing. It's terrible, but that's the sort of thing I remember."

Bono also admitted, "I remember the trees outside the back of the house where we lived, and them tearing those trees down to build an awful development. I remember real anger."[1]

That might seem a surprisingly turbulent confession from a man who was named *Time* magazine's Person of the Year for 2005, along with Bill and Melinda Gates, for his humanitarian work. In spite of his background, filled with such anger, Bono was able to make radical changes in his life, it would appear, for he's now made it his cause to help AIDS victims in Africa.

Because of the consistency factor, it would be easy for Bono to lash out from that foundation of anger he felt in his childhood. The little boy that Bono once was, he still is, so part of the lie from his early childhood memories might be that acting out in anger would in some way solve his frustrations with what's happening around him. Though he may still feel a propensity to lash out—I don't know—instead he seems to have severed ties to that frustrated private logic and is now living a different life that embraces hope rather than the retaliation that once caused him to bash a kid's head into a railing.

One Catholic priest who has been following U2 for decades said this of one of the band's most beloved songs, "Where the Streets Have No Name":

The band has commented that whenever they play this song live, they feel the power of God present in the concert. People might have expected that "peaceniks" like U2 would have ranted and raved about the evils of . . . U.S. foreign policy and war. Rather, they presented an incredible, Christian view of hope. They didn't counter anger with more anger.[2]

Unless you're somehow radically different from the 6 billion others of us on this planet, you too are telling yourself lies that affect the way you see yourself in relation to your environment and those around you. As you understand your lifestyle, do you see how your childhood memories shed light on why you do some of the things you wish you didn't do?

But now for the big step. What are you going to do about it?

After writing down or discussing three to five childhood memories with a friend (see page 88 in chapter 6), ask yourself the following questions:

- As I look at my memories, do I suspect there may be a lie in there somewhere? If so, what is it?
- Do those memories have any direct relationship to how I live my life today? If so, how?
- Does the private logic in my memories keep me from moving ahead in my life? If so, how? Get specific.

You see, the choice is up to you. You can stay in the same rut or you can begin to make changes. You can take the plunge and begin seeking the truth about yourself and your place in the world, or you can stay with what's comfortable and familiar.

So, what'll it be?

Charlie Brown's Illogical Private Logic

I'll admit, Charlie Brown had it pretty rough. The poor guy couldn't win a baseball game to save his life. He always wound up flat on his back when trying to kick the football that Lucy pulled out from under him. And the object of his affection, the little red-haired girl, was always just out of reach. (Though I can't imagine that she was too impressed by the fact that he wore the same old striped shirt day after day.)

Charles Schulz, creator of the beloved Peanuts cartoon that ran for half a century, based Charlie Brown's character on some of his own Charlie Brownish experiences growing up. His cartoon sketches were all rejected by the editors of his high school yearbook—even after his teacher suggested he submit them![3] Another time, a local movie theater promised chocolate bars to the first one hundred kids in line.[4]

Guess what number Schulz was?

Perhaps you, too, feel like that 101st child who always just misses out on the chocolate bar no matter what you do. You always seem to end up flat on your back, losing the game, and missing out on the love of your life. String together a bunch of those experiences and you may find yourself walking around with slumped shoulders, kicking the dirt with the rest of the Charlie Browns of this world.

Many of you, as you look back at your memories, will find that you recall negative experience after negative experience—in fact, more negative memories than positive ones. *Why don't I have very many positive memories?* you may wonder. *Surely I had positive experiences growing up as well as negative ones.*

Why don't some of you more readily remember the positive experiences? Remember the consistency factor? If your childhood memories are predominantly negative, it's because your positive experiences and successes were not consistent with how you saw yourself as a child—and quite likely how you see yourself today. Perhaps your parents were always looking beyond your kindergarten finger paintings to your "greater potential" in the future's advanced-placement tests. Or they were discussing the "big picture" of your reading progress in second grade rather than affirming your grade of 93 percent on the first week's spelling quiz.

Consequently, even when you did well, you received the message that you were falling short of your parents' expectations. In turn, this created much higher expectations in you, and you began to focus on the negative things you did that you felt undermined your parents' expectations. The negatives they saw in your life, you began to view as negatives as well.

Another reason many people remember more negative than positive memories is that there are statistically more firstborn children and only children than any other birth order in the average American family, and those children are the ones most likely to spot a flaw. Therefore, the majority of you are more likely to focus on negative memories than on positive ones. Middleborn and lastborn children may have negative memories, but those generally aren't the first memories that come to mind. Their private logic may eventually be shaped by their family environment to focus on negative memories, but my guess is that they would more naturally begin life with more positive memories regarding themselves—receiving a star for a project at school, winning a race, or building a model that everyone loves. So unless a lastborn's parents were extremely critical, he or she is not going to have as many negative memories.

Finally, our society today simply emphasizes negative experiences, dwelling on what's wrong rather than on what's right. Just ask most high school juniors on the honor roll what their fathers say when they bring a report card home with six As and a B+.

"Hey, what's with the B+?!"

Negative thinking permeates our society and, consequently, breeds people whose negative private logic causes them to define themselves not by their strengths but by their weaknesses—many of which are further distorted by their own interpretations.

I offer that caution especially to firstborn and only children, as well as to any children whose parents were extremely critical. Evaluate your collection of early childhood memories. If you see more negative than positive memories, then be especially vigilant in not being hyper-critical yourself, because you will have a greater tendency to emphasize the negative experiences in life. While a critical eye is a nice trait to have if you're a risk-management lawyer, a renowned portrait photographer, or an auditor for the IRS, it's generally a "talent" that you have to manage carefully so as not to mow down everyone in your path!

What's Real? What's Perception?

Like that "mountain" that my mother and I pulled the Radio Flyer wagon up on the way to the grocery store, in my childhood mind the church that my family attended rivaled St. Peter's Basilica in Rome for sheer size. I remember it as being cavernous, with seating for hundreds. A kid could get lost in a place like that.

Or so I thought.

Decades later, I had the opportunity to speak in that same church where I had crawled around on the floor, switching women's shoes. But as I walked in, there was a rush of both familiarity and bewilderment. Sure, I was in the right place, but very few things were precisely the way I remembered them. Even when I was in front of the audience speaking, an incredulous voice in the back of my mind kept saying over and over, *This place is so small!* Finally, I couldn't help but count the pews—all ten on each side. Ten! Somehow, over the years, that "cathedral" had shrunk and been crossed off the pope's tour circuit. As the truth sank in, I came to terms with the fact that it had always been small. The difference was simply between how I saw it as a child and how I saw it as an adult.

It's probably safe to say that every one of our memories is distorted in some way or another by our flawed perceptions. Some psychologists even point out that the precise way we recall our memories shifts throughout our lives, so that you remember crashing your bike into the curb as a young child somewhat differently when you're 14 years old than when you're 27, and differently when you're 53.[5] And sometimes, on occasion, the things you remember may never even have happened.

Binjamin Wilkomirski's memoir, *Fragments: Memories of a War-time Childhood*, recounts his so-called boyhood experiences of living through the Holocaust in a concentration camp. Allegedly, he didn't "remember" these experiences until they were uncovered in therapy as an adult. But when a Swiss journalist revealed that Binjamin Wilkomirski was actually born to Yvonne Grosjean and given up to an orphanage, where he was adopted by the Dössekkers and named Bruno, the story fell apart. Bruno had, in fact, spent the World War II years safely in Switzerland. But, unlike some stories of blatantly contrived "journalism," Wilkomirski/Dössekker still believes the events truly happened to him.[6]

I'm not saying that traumatic memories can't be buried deep in your psyche and uncovered later by therapy. They certainly can. I'm simply pointing out that sometimes what you remember not only didn't happen the way you remember it, but it may have never happened at all.

> Sometimes what you remember not only didn't happen the way you remember it, but it may have never happened at all.

It's a controversial topic, I know. But whether or not the experience stored in your memory actually happened—as terribly important as that question is—is not my point. My point is that if you have a painful memory of an event that in fact never happened—or that didn't happen in nearly the same way you remember it—the message of your fictitious memory still speaks loudly and clearly about your private logic and lifestyle. As misguided as it is to concoct a memory from thin air, that perspective through which you interpreted your concocted memory is telling you in no uncertain terms how you see life.

If you're able to revisit your childhood memories—whether in person as I did by visiting my childhood church or imaginatively by thinking back—you'll begin to see how you make all kinds of leaps in perception between the feelings you associated with the memory and the facts of the experience itself.

What's That You Say?

We all tell ourselves lies at some point. No one is immune. We lie to ourselves about our health (*I'm not that overweight.*). We lie to ourselves about our work habits (*If I don't work overtime and do the job myself, no one in the office will ever get the job done right.*). And we lie to ourselves about our relationships (*If it weren't for his issues, we'd be doing great!*).

115

You've probably walked or driven downtown and seen a disheveled, homeless person on the street, talking to himself. It's easy to turn the other way and shake your head at that kind of behavior without realizing that you, too, go through life mumbling to yourself about what you're angry about or what you feel the world has done to you. You may not speak those messages out loud (at least around anybody else), but you certainly speak them inside. The truth is that you're not so different from that man on the street because we all engage in self-talk. Self-talk is simply the voice of your private logic inside responding to what happens around you. And it responds either graciously and truthfully . . . or condemningly with lies.

With all those lies bouncing around inside your head, you're bound to get turned around on occasion. For some people, that voice inside is always "should-ing" them, telling them exactly where they went wrong, how they should have performed, and giving them a 10-point outline of precisely how inept they really are. *You idiot*, the voice says, *you should've known better than to leave during rush-hour traffic!* For others, that voice lets them get away with all sorts of behavior. *I know I'm on a diet, but what difference is one more bowl of ice cream really going to make? I give myself so few rewards anyway.*

The question is, What is your self-talk saying? Is that little voice helping you, graciously pointing out the truth where you need to change and encouraging you on? Or is it discouraging you and tearing you down?

Ladies, imagine that a man you met at your friend's wedding arranges to meet you for coffee on Saturday morning. You get there twenty minutes early and wait anxiously for him to show up. But he doesn't arrive and you continue waiting for an hour and a half after your scheduled meeting time before you finally leave, dejected.

What's the self-talk going on inside you?

You might be berating yourself for having talked as much as you did when the two of you talked over wedding cake. Or you might be beating your head against the wall as to why you played it so cool when he really seemed like a nice guy. Why didn't you tell him you enjoyed his company?

But what should your self-talk be?

The truth about that situation is that the guy promised to do something and didn't follow through. Frankly, if he's that kind of a guy, who needs him anyway?

But if the message running in a continuous loop through your head points the blame at yourself (*I always get let down. What's wrong with me?*), you're believing a lie. If your self-talk is healthy—if you are recognizing your weaknesses and handling them graciously—the lies in your private logic and lifestyle can't "talk back."

> There are two kinds of people in the world: those who tell themselves lies and believe them. And those who tell themselves lies but choose to fight them.

There are two kinds of people in the world: those who tell themselves lies and believe them, and those who tell themselves lies but choose to fight them.

Which kind of person are you?

As Pinocchio found out, you don't move forward in life to becoming the real person you were created to be until you face those lies in your life. Sadly, my experience from talking with people all over the country is that most of them never tackle the lies they tell themselves. They remain stuck in their ruts, telling themselves another lie: that it's too difficult to change and not worth the effort anyway.

Those people are so wrong. You can change, and the effort is so worth it! Not only for you personally, but for the loved ones, coworkers, friends, and acquaintances in your present and on into your future.

But how can you start making that change?

117

Speak the truth to yourself in love.

Have you ever ordered something in a restaurant that didn't turn out the way you asked for it?

While my wife, Sande, and I were at a restaurant for a special occasion, I noticed that she was picking at her salmon like a four-year-old picking at lima beans.

"Are you enjoying your dinner?" I asked.

"Oh, yes . . . ," she said.

But after a few minutes I knew something wasn't right.

"Are you sure your dinner is okay?" I asked again.

"Well," she said, almost embarrassed, "it is a bit undercooked."

Undercooked was an understatement. I nearly had to bonk the fish over the head to keep it from jumping into my water glass. When I notified the maître d', he was horrified and sent Sande's fish back into the kitchen faster than a barracuda, and a new entrée was out in no time.

You tell me what's the respectful thing to do in a situation like that? I think that the respectful thing is to hold the cook and wait staff accountable for the way you order the food. If you order a steak medium well and it comes out mooing, the reasonable thing to do is to send it back to pasture for a little more time.

Speaking the truth in love requires two parts—truth and love. Cut either one out of the equation, and you'll cut yourself short. You may be one of the most difficult people for you to love because you know your weaknesses so well. Likewise, you may be one of the most difficult people to tell the truth to because it's so much easier to avoid facing the lies you tell yourself.

But put those two elements together in your life—truth and love—and see how much easier they are to take!

Realize you'll sometimes take three steps forward and two steps back.
No matter how motivated you are to seek the truth about the lies you tell yourself, no matter how much you want to allow your private logic and lifestyle to be reshaped, I think it's only fair that I tell you what lies down the road a few steps.

You're going to fail.

Yup, you read *that* right. And by saying this, I don't mean to discourage you. In fact, quite the opposite—I mean that as an encouragement!

Well, if your intention was to encourage me, Dr. Leman, you might be thinking, *you sure chose a peculiar way to go about it.*

But here's what I mean. I'm simply giving you permission to fail as you change those aspects of your private logic and lifestyle that hold you back. Perhaps you were shy growing up, so you've made a conscious point of initiating conversations in social situations. Or you've decided that you're not going to steamroll over your spouse when he leaves his dirty clothes hanging on the bedroom doorknob again. Or, if you're a parent, you and your husband agree that you're never going to raise your voices at your children like your own parents did. Instead you're going to use time-outs and consequences to correct your children's poor behavior.

Still, I'll tell you with certainty that there will come a time when life is closing in on you, and you'll feel the urge to retreat to that shy little child you once were, lash out at your spouse again the way your family did, and not only use the same words with your child that your own father or mother used with you, but also with the same tone and inflection (maybe even with added vigor).

Because of the consistency factor, it's not easy to escape the lies you tell yourself. The little boy or girl that you once were built the foundation for your private logic, and that child is still clinging to your leg everywhere you go. By facing the lies of your private logic and lifestyle, you're doing the difficult work of replacing parts of that foundation you've grown up with and upon which your thoughts, decisions, and actions are formed.

Don't get me wrong. You can change, but when push comes to shove, you're still apt to return to those childhood patterns. So an important part of truth therapy, which we'll examine in more detail in the next chapter, is recognizing that from time to time you're going to slip back into your early, ingrained behavior. Your course will always be a meandering one as you set out, slide back into familiar patterns, and then reorient yourself and get back on track. You don't have to be subject to your past. You can change as you step into the future. But be aware that with negative imprinting in your life, you're usually going to make progress with three steps forward and two steps back. Sometimes you'll even take seven or eight steps back. But don't worry. That happens to everybody. As long as you pick yourself up, dust yourself off, and continue moving in the right direction, three steps forward and two steps back is still a step in the right direction.

The question then is, what direction are you heading in? What course are you faithful to, no matter how blown off course you are at times? To make sure that for every two steps backward you're still taking three steps in the right direction, find benchmarks to remind you that you're making progress, that you're on the right track and working toward being a good person, a good spouse, and a good parent.

Notice that I said good person, not a perfect person. If you're

119

always striving to be perfect, you're setting yourself up for failure. So why not cut yourself some slack? Watch your expectations and don't be too self-critical. Doctors who help people manage their weight will tell them not to weigh themselves every day. Why? Because every person's weight fluctuates. They don't want you to get discouraged. Weigh yourself once a week and if you must have an expectation, let it be that you'll lose a pound. One pound—that's it!

> If you're always striving to be perfect, you're setting yourself up for failure.

Diet experts will tell you that ideal weight loss is a pound to a pound and a half per week. That's the ideal. Yet headlines of magazines in the grocery aisle scream things such as "300-Pound Woman Now Wears a Size 2!" and "I Lost 50 Pounds in One Month!" Sure, that's possible if you're open to the lose-a-leg diet. But, hey, you know what they say: "No pain, no gain!"

Unfortunately, we live in an instant Jell-O society, with everybody wanting microwaved success. So as you look at truth therapy to combat the lies you tell yourself, don't go overboard with your expectations.

Remember to lighten up and put your party hat on every now and then. Celebrate the little steps . . . as well as the significant milestones.

Life's a Party—and You're Invited!

In keeping with my lastborn fun-loving trait, I like to tell people that there's a party happening right in front of your eyes. It's called life! The party hats are out, the cake's being cut, and the noisemakers are screaming out full blast.

Do you plan on showing up?

I ask because many people have a hard time joining in. Subconsciously they give all kinds of excuses why they can't make it. They tell themselves there's too much work to be done. Or they don't feel they deserve to join the party because they're too busy being martyrs so others can enjoy life. So many people I know mope around, waiting for life to get better.

But who says you can't come to the party? That voice of your negative self-talk? Your parents? Your spouse or friends?

As we head into the next chapter, I'm extending to you a wonderful invitation: Combat your lies with the truth and join the party called life! Don't miss out!

Avoiding the Wasted Years

The ABCs of truth therapy

It's unusual for older couples to seek counseling, so when a husband and wife in their sixties, who had been married well over forty years, approached me to talk about the problems they were having in their marriage, their ages immediately set them apart from the majority of people who have sat across from me in my counseling office. The fact that they showed wisdom in seeking counseling together gave me great hope for their marriage, in spite of the fact that in my office they fought like a pair of two-year-olds.

As I probed for the root of their problem, the wife finally blurted out that she felt she was always being compared to her mother-in-law. That isn't a particularly uncommon experience for wives, but what made hers different was that her mother-in-law had been dead for twenty years. Talk about holding a grudge!

To prove her point, she dredged up from memory, repeating word-for-word something her husband had said decades ago in comparing her with her mother-in-law. Those few words had wounded her deeply. The wedge that had been driven between the two of them strained their verbal communication, their sexual intimacy—the list went on and on. Her husband had dismissed her as being cold, but she was anything but cold. She was fiery with anger and kept that anger simmering beneath the surface like a volcano preparing for the big blowup. And the kicker? For more than twenty years, she had never told him how she felt.

Instances such as that one led me to use the term "the wasted years." So many people, by letting pain from past memories grow into lies that choke the present and twist their future, waste years. Not weeks—years!—by holding on to a grudge against others. But as those two were finally able to express their hurts, listen, offer their forgiveness, and reaffirm their love to each other, they embraced. It was one of the most tender moments in my counseling office to watch that couple who began our sessions so far apart come together and tell each other that they loved each other, something they hadn't said in years.

Like most couples, they had a happy beginning. And, because of their renewed understanding of each other, they would most likely have a happy ending. But stop for a moment and think about that not-so-happy middle. Think of what was wasted over the years—the walks they could have taken together hand in hand, the words of love and affirmation that could have deepened over the years, the intimate talks. All that was squelched because of a harbored sentence spoken in another era.

What a waste!

Scripture, that age-old book of wisdom, says, "Do not let the sun go down while you are still angry."[1] I imagine that as the apostle Paul wrote those words, he probably had people in mind very much like that husband and wife. If you allow your anger against others to bleed into the next day and then the next and so on, your relationships, your outlook on life, and your own soul will quickly be poisoned.

For those of you who have childhood memories with pain or loss in them, it probably doesn't take much to recall those grievances and grudges. But as we look at the power of confronting the truth about your past, I hope that you, like that couple, can avoid the waste before days turn into weeks, weeks turn into months, and months turn into years. You can take control. You can avoid those wasted years.

And it's never too late to start.

A Different Kind of ABCs

I admire that couple so much for valuing each other enough to risk opening the pain they felt inside, for being willing to be humble and to understand their spouse's point of view—and ultimately to live differently based on the truth. By doing what they did, they embraced what I call the ABCs of truth therapy.

They were willing to accept that their memories were inaccurate—in other words, that the experiences they each remembered could have been interpreted by others in a different way.

They put in the hard work of believing the truth about their memories by setting aside their own presumptions and listening to another's perspective.

Finally, they changed their behavior by going forward based on the truth.

The process that couple went through is the same process you can go through as you look at your childhood memories and begin to understand your private logic and lifestyle themes. By walking through these three steps, you too can change the way you understand yourself and your memories.

You can face memories in which others have hurt you or in which you feel you haven't measured up in life.

You can get perspective on your memories outside of your private logic, then believe the truth rather than the lies about them.

You can change your behavior by adopting a new response to your memories.

And that makes for a much healthier lifestyle and a happier you!

Accept the truth. Your memories are inaccurate.
If that hill between my house and the grocery store seemed so enormous, or if details in your own memories were quite literally larger than life, then don't you think that other parts of your memories could be lying as well? It happens perhaps more than you realize. Our

The ABCs of Truth Therapy

Accept that your memories are inaccurate.
Believe the truth about your memories.
Change your behavior based on the truth.

daughter Holly recently shared one of her childhood memories with the rest of the family, but she remembered only part of it correctly. For one, it didn't happen in Arizona, as she recalled (it happened in New York), and she also didn't have the sequence of events correct.

Accepting that your memories may be lying might seem like a given after all we've talked about, but don't underestimate this foundation of truth therapy. Failing to start from here is like a person visiting an Alcoholics Anonymous meeting for help, but refusing to admit that he has a drinking problem. If you are going to discover the truth about your memories, you have to start by acknowledging that, yes, your psyche does indeed select experiences for your memory bank that are consistent with how you view life and that your interpretations of those events are formed, and possibly skewed, by your own private logic.

Once you've taken that first step of accepting that your memories may be lying, you're ready to replace the lies with something else: the truth.

Believe the truth about your memories.
Objectively identifying the truth about yourself can be about as easy as looking at the back of your own head. If your private logic continually slips subtle lies to you, how are you ever going to uncover what's true and what's not?

That's why you can't do it alone. And why I suggest that in addition to looking backward from time to time to see how far you've come, you find others to help reflect back to you the truth about the way you live. To get an objective perspective on yourself, you're going to need help.

It's almost comical, isn't it, how different witnesses can give completely different stories as to what happened at a traffic accident? One person says that the southbound car signaled left and didn't stop before turning in front of the northbound car. Another says that it did stop before turning. Still another claims that the real problem was that the northbound car was speeding. No, says a fourth witness, the northbound car was not speeding.

How can anyone ever make sense of all this?

The fact is, all four witnesses' accounts may be true if you dig deeply enough into their stories and perspectives. Perhaps the driver did signal and the car came to a near stop before turning in front of the other car heading north. One witness's definition of "coming to a stop" may be different than another's, so that both witnesses saw the same event but had different interpretations of the driver's intentions and actions. Likewise, what a 17-year-old driver calls speeding may look completely different from what a 77-year-old driver calls speeding.

The same is true of your childhood memories. Everyone in your family is going to have slightly—if not radically—different interpretations of the same event. It all goes back to the unique private logic that each person has and the different ways you and others interpret your family environment.

Let's say that when you were growing up your family went to your grandparents' house every Thanksgiving holiday. You may remember those trips brimming over with stress as everyone rushed frantically around the house to get packed and into the car with full suitcases and empty bladders. You may also distinctly recall feeling uncomfortable at your grandparents' house because Granddad was in the early stages of Alzheimer's and "acted funny."

Your younger sister, however, may have loved the buzz of excitement as everyone got ready for the trip. She may have relished the thrill of everyone gathering in one place, eating so much great food, and playing silly games with Granddad.

Your father may have loved the break of getting out to see his in-laws, but your mother may have dreaded those four days because of all the unresolved issues it brought up between her and her parents.

For some of you then, Thanksgiving memories were great. For others they weren't so great. All of you were there for the same events, so what makes the difference? Again, because of each person's private logic, most likely the real "state of the union" for your family probably lies somewhere in the middle. To help you get closer to the truth about the interpretations and feelings you hold about your past and the way you see yourself in relation to others, I recommend the following activity.

Sometime when your family is together bring up one or two of your childhood memories. I'm not suggesting that you call a family summit meeting to "get to the bottom of your memories," but bring a memory up casually. If a few of you are riding in a car or if you're all sitting around a dinner table somewhere, you might say something such as, "You know, I was thinking back to those times when we all went to Grandma and Granddad's for Thanksgiving. Do you remember that?" Usually that's all that's needed to open the conversation.

"Oh, I still think about those trips every Thanksgiving," your younger sister might say. "I really miss those trips."

"Really?" someone else might say. "How come? Because what I remember is. . . ."

You might be surprised how easy it is to get people to share how they felt about those events. If you find that a specific memory is hurtful for someone, then it's probably not a good idea to press the matter in a group setting. Instead raise the subject privately when the opportunity presents itself. That act of sharing memories together as a family fills in the gaps in your own interpretations and feelings. If you dreaded those Thanksgiving holidays, hearing your little sister's love of them may help you see that maybe they weren't so bad after all. If those four days in November were all fun and games for you, hearing that there was tension rumbling just beneath the surface might also help you get a better grip on reality, because those contrasting interpretations from family members often help bring balance to your interpretations.

Sharing childhood memories as a family isn't a foolproof way to the truth, of course, because we all carry our share of foolishness! All families have their own sometimes-illogical system of relating to one another, so in some ways you'll all be sharing a common, partially distorted private logic. Your family may value silence and outward composure over the truth, they may value expressing their feelings over the facts, or they may all value receiving negative attention in ways that distort any attempt at sharing honestly together. In some families, sharing childhood memories can even take you down some rather exasperating roads!

> Sharing memories together as a family fills in the gaps in your own interpretations and feelings.

The value of this exercise depends in part on the maturity of your family members, so don't expect perfect insight into your life. Still, if you approach the discussion casually and take the messages you receive from family members with a grain of salt, you'll find that three or four heads or, in the case of our family, seven heads really are better than one!

As you get people's input, however, I want to caution you about one thing: Beware that your friends don't perpetuate your lies. Have you ever been in a coffee shop or restaurant where, as much as you would have liked to escape the conversation next to you, you couldn't help but be dragged through the innermost details of someone else's life? Not only can it be downright embarrassing, sometimes it can be like witnessing the blind leading the blind.

I was once sitting in a restaurant about three feet from two women, one of whom was telling her friend in detail about her boyfriend's sexual indiscretions with her. Having been pulled into their public confessional booth, I didn't have much difficulty seeing that this guy was interested in just one thing—and it wasn't his girlfriend's thoughts on solving world poverty.

"Oh, you poor thing!" the other woman kept saying over and over, giving her friend all sorts of emotional payoff that she shouldn't have been receiving for her lack of foresight. Rather than being remotely helpful and saying something such as, "Umm . . . it sounds to me like he's using you," or "Maybe you shouldn't be seeing him," or "Have you thought of dating other guys—someone who will respect you more?" the so-called friend kept nodding like a dashboard bobble-head doll. The two of them finished their salads and went their separate ways, but that "friend" didn't help one bit simply because she didn't speak the truth.

Getting others' perspectives on the way you approach life is not only worthwhile, I believe it's essential. I have a couple male friends that I've come to trust over the years and can talk to about anything— and I mean anything! As you assess your childhood memories and begin to discover the potential weaknesses in your private logic and lifestyle themes, think about who that trusted person is in your life. Who truly loves and cares about you, no strings attached? If you have such a person in your life, go to him or her and say, "Hey, I could use your help. Would you shoot it to me straight? Why do you think I'm always overbooking myself? Am I trying to please others too much?"

Make sure, though, that your close friends are willing to tell you the truth in love. They need to provide an objective sounding board to help you see where you might need to change, as well as where you might be blind to the truth about yourself.

One final point—and it's an important one. Sharing your life with a trusted friend is wise, but baring your soul to everybody is foolish.

If you flaunt your problems, trying to get attention from anyone willing to listen for half a minute during the neighborhood play group, in the grocery store line, or anywhere else you can find an open ear . . . well, let's say it straight. Eventually no one will want to be around you. Worse still, in the event that you do find someone—that bobble-headed yes man (or woman)—willing to go through the motions with you to feed their own need for attention, you truly will become the blind leading the blind. If all either of you does is unload problems on the other or encourage foolish behavior, after a while, who needs it? It'll only serve to sink you both deeper into your ruts.

131

Change your behavior based on the truth.

You change the oil in your car every three to six months, and you change the batteries in your home's smoke detectors every half year, but changing your behavior takes quite a bit more doing. You can accept that your memories and private logic are lying to you. You can objectively seek the truth. But exactly how do you go about changing your behavior?

That, dear reader, is the million-dollar question, and of the three steps in truth therapy, changing your behavior is the most difficult. The answer requires patience, perseverance, and grace.

Remember the movie *What About Bob?* starring comedian Bill Murray? In the movie, psychiatrist Dr. Leo Marvin has just published a book called *Baby Steps.* His premise is that one key to making major changes in your life involves taking baby steps and celebrating your incremental progress.

You know, coming from a fictionalized, big-screen shrink, that's not half-bad advice. There's real truth to his book's premise! If you are able to slowly but surely put one foot in front of the other, no matter how small your steps are, you'll soon find yourself heading down the road toward change.

If you've followed the principles I've covered so far and you're ready to confront the lies in your private logic and lifestyle to change your behavior, good for you! I'm so proud of your initiative. You're doing the right thing by committing to make changes. So many people continue in the rut they've been in for decades and look to anyone for change except that person staring back at them in the mirror. They use their doctor-prescribed pills as a crutch. They sign up for hypnosis. They want "three easy steps to a new you" and expect to arrive halfway through step one. The reality is that to make significant change, you need to alter how you view life.

> To make significant change, you need to alter how you view life.

But that doesn't happen overnight! It means holding on to your enthusiasm and perseverance but letting go of any unreasonable expectations. Significant, lasting change takes time—lots of it. But remember that every cross-country journey begins with a few steps. A flight to the moon begins by the rocket inching upward, fighting gravity. Construction of the world's tallest skyscrapers starts with the first shovelful of dirt. No matter how committed you are to changing your behavior, it's going to take time—and you can either fight or choose to accept that reality.

Your assignment, therefore, is to recognize and celebrate when you see yourself making those small changes. If your private logic tells you that you need to maintain peace in your relationships at all costs, a small change might be gently pointing out to the grocery store cashier that you've been shortchanged. If your private logic is that of a martyr, you might politely decline the invitation to bail out your sister again. If you are a controller, a small change might be asking your coworker what she thinks is the best solution to a problem. Give yourself the grace to take those three baby steps forward and two steps back—and at times two steps forward and three steps back.

Remember, small change adds up!

Every now and then, don't forget to look back to see how far you've come. When my ancestors arrived in America from Ireland, they didn't step off the boat wearing tailored Armani suits. The Lemans were poor Irish immigrants for whom meager was a pretty generous word to describe their standard of living. My father used to tell a story about himself and his three brothers, who had only a year in age between each of them. Money was so tight in their family, he said, that whoever got out of bed first was the best dressed that day because that person got the pick of which clothes to wear.

I like looking at those old photo albums of my Leman forefathers to remind me where I've come from. That's a good practice wherever you are in life! So, from time to time, I encourage you to stop and look back to see how far you've come. When I play golf and thwack the little white ball off the tee, my best shot might not look like much. But when I hike down the fairway, find my ball in the grass (often rather tall grass!), and glance back at the tee, it always appears as if it's traveled farther than I thought. I might check to see if my golfing partners are impressed, because occasionally I impress myself. *Wow, did you really hit it that far?* I sometimes think, observing my ball to make sure I've got the right one. *Not bad, Leman.*

> Look back every now and then to see how far you've already come.

If you walk through life believing that your steps aren't getting you anywhere, by looking back every now and then you'll see that you've come farther than you thought. On the other hand, if you think more of yourself than perhaps you ought to, looking back can help you refocus on reality. Some people exaggerate their progress, while others downplay theirs. Occasionally reviewing your private logic and lifestyle themes revealed in your childhood memories provides you with a reference point to assess how you've changed and to keep you moving in a positive direction.

I believe life doesn't get more difficult as you continue moving ahead. It gets easier.

What Do Feelings Have to Do with It?

Decades ago a popular mantra in our culture was "If it feels good, do it." The contemporary spin on that message—one that so many believe today, whether consciously or unconsciously—is "I have to be true to what I feel." Both, however, are lies that would have you believe that your feelings call the shots regarding your behavior. But that's often putting the proverbial cart in front of the horse. If I always followed my feelings I'd probably have run more than a few people off the highway, and if I always waited for my feelings to motivate me before I acted, I'd spend an awful lot of time on the couch twiddling my thumbs for a wave of charity to hit me. Always following your feelings simply isn't wise.

I bring that up because any significant change to your private logic almost always precedes your feelings. It's like a large ship responding to your steering. You may decide to navigate a new course and turn the ship's wheel to the port side, but the boat will take a minute or two to change directions. It's the same with your feelings. An awareness of your private logic will help you as you respond in social situations. You'll know how you typically respond, and you can begin catching yourself and choosing to respond differently. But while you may choose to be more outgoing, you most likely won't feel any different when you first go out of your way to initiate conversations. Once you begin behaving differently, however, you'll find that, over time, your feelings will begin to fall in line.

Panning for the Gold of Your Positive Memories

If you're a firstborn child or an only child with an eagle eye for spotting flaws at one hundred paces and you find yourself unable to recall any positive memories, don't despair. Or perhaps you've come from a family with critical parents and you've grown into a hypercritical person yourself. *Don't give up on trying to change.*

Searching for glimmers of positive memories in your past may feel like sifting through mountains of gravel and sand, panning for a speck of gold. You may be weary to the bone from having tried to overcome the gravel of your own weaknesses and may feel that from all you've experienced and reflected upon in your past, "there ain't no gold in them thar hills." But the gold is there if you're willing to dig through your memories. When you find that gold nugget gleaming up at you from the pan after all your hard work, all that gravel of your past will begin to fade into the background!

135

When I started a fruit stand in front of our house when I was growing up, I was pretty enterprising. I even sold bags of dirt door to door. (It takes the kind of salesman who can sell refrigerators to Eskimos to pull that off!) Yet when I compared myself to my older brother and sister on the fast track to sainthood, I began believing the lie that I was a dummy. That's why when my geometry teacher, Ms. Wilson, pulled me aside and asked, "Did you ever consider that you could use the skills you have to do something worthwhile in life?" it was like being pointed toward a vein of gold.

Skills? I thought. *What skills?* No one ever told me I had skills.

Changing your behavior involves changing your private logic, your outlook on life—and that is one of the most difficult things to change. It's easier for most people to remember the negative events from their past than the positive ones, and people tend to perpetuate their view of themselves by holding on to their negative ways of looking at the world. I probably would have gone on thinking that I was a dummy if Ms. Wilson and others hadn't pointed me in the direction of gold.

Even though negative experiences may vastly outnumber the positive ones in your past, you do have positive experiences stored in your memory that gave you real joy in life. Tap into those, and you'll find a key to the real, positively motivated, forward-looking you. Ask yourself, "What gave me joy when I was young? What made me feel good?"

For many of you, that should trigger such memories as "When I was eight I started gymnastics and really enjoyed it. I made a lot of friends there and—oh, yeah!—I remember people clapping after I performed my gymnastics routine at the end of the season."

Or "Let's see . . . when I was nine, that was my first year in Little League baseball. I remember that they only kept two nine-year-olds on the team, and I was one of them. I felt pretty good about that."

So even if the majority of your childhood memories at first seem negative, dig deep to find those positive memories and what they say about you. Ask yourself the following questions:

- When I think of my childhood and having fun, what pops into my mind . . . no matter how insignificant it seems at first?
- What did I do as a kid that was considerate to others?

Look back to when you were between five and ten years old. Is there anybody you knew then who really gave you joy? Who brightened your day whenever you were around him or her? Why did you respond that way?

What's the first thing that pops into your mind when you think of having fun? For some of you, it might be mischievous fun that comes to mind, such as sneaking out of bed at night and going downstairs to rob the cookie jar—but nevertheless that's what felt fun to you at the time.

Also explore your positive memories that don't come as readily to mind. If you dig deep enough you'll unearth some real treasures that can give you clues to your positive strengths. While your memories of building your tree fort or creating a tea party with your best friend for your dolls might not be as easy to recall as the time you tripped on your shoelace and broke your glasses on the school playground, those positive memories that you've stored also hold clues to who you are. You may not readily remember sneaking into the kitchen at midnight for a chocolate-chip cookie or the thrill you felt at entertaining your parents and your father's work colleagues after dinner with your impromptu play, but you enjoyed them for a reason, didn't you? Those positive memories will have something to say about who you are and reveal an aspect of your personality that may have sat dormant for far too many years—such as the ability to create, the desire to entertain others . . . even the satisfaction of putting a plan into action and pulling it off.

It might take some thought, but that work will yield you gold!

Now You Know Your ABCs . . .

Can you remember struggling through your ABCs as a child? Your preschool and kindergarten teachers probably helped you by teaching you the alphabet song and wallpapering the classroom with colorful pictures of everything from apples to zebras. It's one thing to learn the alphabet, however, and another thing entirely to put those letters to use forming words, and then stringing words together to form sentences in order to read and write. Perhaps if you'd known way back in kindergarten how much trouble it was going to be, you might have packed up your nap-time mat, fixed a paper plate of cookies and milk for the road, and headed out of that classroom.

If all you ever learned were the 26 letters of the alphabet without applying them further, what would have been the use? But as insurmountable as learning to read may have seemed to you then as a little ankle-biter, look at you now, working your way through this book. Likewise, now that you know the ABCs of truth therapy—accepting that your memories may be lying, believing the truth about them, and changing your behavior—what are you going to do with those pieces? How will you step toward change?

Perhaps the truth of your positive memories has been stored away far too long because of the way you see yourself. Perhaps you've been through a seemingly endless string of difficult circumstances in life or you still feel anger toward your parents for painful childhood memories you have. Whatever the difficulties you've faced, you can overcome the lies attached to your private logic that continue to hold you back.

> Whatever the difficulties you've faced, you can overcome the lies attached to your private logic that continue to hold you back.

So many people look everywhere but to themselves for the change that needs to happen in their lives, pointing at their missed opportunities and blaming their parents.

You don't have to be one of them.

Instead, continue to seize the opportunities before you to embrace the truth. Take steps toward letting your parents off the hook (something we'll talk about in detail in the next chapter). If you do, I think you'll find that those can be some of the most freeing steps you'll ever take.

Escaping the Parent Trap

You can change your painful memories

Maria was in her midthirties and had been married for 15 years when she first visited me to discuss some problems in her relationship with her husband. To put it bluntly, she was ready to call it quits on sex altogether. After Maria and I talked a while, I discovered that her marital problems were really a manifestation of the sexual abuse she had experienced at a young age. To make matters more difficult, the perpetrator was her own father, who still lived nearby.

At the time we began her therapy, Maria's oldest daughter was 12—the same age Maria had been when her father began to abuse her. Horrific memories of her father entering her bedroom to fondle her and force her to engage in oral sex were rushing back. He had "prepared her" for sex by introducing her to pornography, and Maria now faced a daily battle against those images that were imprinted upon her mind. What made the incest even more terrible was that it continued through high school and into her university years when she remained at home. In fact, it continued almost until the day she was married in her early twenties, although Maria continued to cover up the secret. As far as anyone else was concerned, her relationship with her father was a normal one.

Nothing could have been farther from the truth.

Understandably, Maria needed constant reassurance that she was loved and respected for who she was as a person, not for the sexual fulfillment she could bring to the man in her life. As the oldest daughter in her family, she had worked hard to make everybody happy. Yet underneath it all she would beat herself up again and again, feeding herself the lie that she was used material.

But Maria had guts. She knew she had fallen into a pit, and she didn't want to remain there. So she came to me for help to begin the climb back out. After hearing everything she'd been through, I deeply admired her initiative.

Over several years in counseling, Maria realized that if she were ever to experience healing, she would need to forgive her father—and that was no small thing. Even more difficult, Maria knew the abuse would have to come out in the open not only with her dad but also with her mom, who couldn't understand why her daughter wouldn't let her grandkids stay with them alone for an hour, much less overnight.

At first Maria couldn't face the idea of confronting her father. But she began the process of forgiving him intellectually when she came to realize that forgiving him didn't mean she was saying that what he had done to her was all right. What he had done was wrong—terribly wrong—and a horrible violation of the trust between a father and a daughter. His abuse had shaped her view of who she was and how she related to all men, and his actions would affect her for a lifetime. Forgiving is not forgetting. Forgiving her father was an active choice not to allow him to maintain his control over her. Forgiving meant that she could then focus on moving ahead with her life instead of being trapped in the past.

Her feelings, however, lagged far behind her intellectual decision to forgive. And who could blame her? Fathers are supposed to protect their daughters, and he had done everything but protect her. When Maria realized how much of her life he had changed by his aberrant sexual behavior, she was angry. Rightfully so!

Also, she was scared to confront her father. Not only did it mean bringing their secret to light and embarrassing him, she was worried about what telling the truth might do to her family—especially her mother, whom she believed knew nothing about the abuse.

It took several years for Maria to confront her parents, but when she did, she did so in a courageous, loving, straightforward way. She began by explaining why she had never allowed her daughters to spend the night at her parents' house. When she had completed her story, her mother was stunned. Her father was livid, angry at being caught. He accused her of lying and being downright crazy. He told her she needed counseling, for all her wild accusations. But as Maria continued, giving specific examples over the years, an understanding and a horror began to grow on her mother's face. Gut-wrenching tears followed.

141

Telling the truth did impact her family. Her parents' marriage was never the same. Her mother forced the father to leave home while they sorted things out. I ended up seeing her mother afterward to help her work through the fallout of discovering what had been behind her husband's occasional strange behavior all those years. Maria and her mother agreed that Maria's siblings also had to know that their father was an abuser for their own and their children's good. One sister yelled at Maria, telling her that she had broken the family apart—that it was her fault. That conversation was heartbreaking for Maria, who loved her sister. But it was not Maria's fault. It was her dad's fault, for he was the one who had done the abusing. Maria was doing the right thing by bringing the truth out into the open. All the grandkids could have been in jeopardy if Maria had kept her secret.

Because Maria stood her ground, in spite of angry siblings and a shocked mother, her father was forced to go into counseling if he ever wanted to return home. And when he chose to do so, there was a new family rule: He was never to be alone with any of the grandchildren, even for a minute. It was the result of his own actions, so he couldn't argue.

It was a difficult several years for Maria. At times she wondered if she could go on. I applaud this courageous woman for taking step after step in a very difficult—and right—direction.

When you feel the pinch of pain from your past, think of Maria. If she could take steps to forgive her father in spite of her debilitating pain and find freedom from the past, then you can too. Your relationship with your parents may not be nearly as traumatic as Maria's. Or it may be even more so. Either way, it is precisely Maria's kind of courage that can help you accept the truth about your relationship with your parents.

You may not be able to change your past or your childhood memories themselves, but you can change the way you understand them and what control they have over your life from here on. You can choose to begin the process of forgiving. You can take one small step at a time, from this day forward.

Are You Locking Yourself in the Past—or Unlocking Your Future?

A classic psychology study was conducted decades ago by Jane Elliott—a third-grade teacher in Riceville, Iowa—who one day began treating blue-eyed children in her class differently, giving them certain special privileges over brown-eyed children.[1] *Well, that's not very politically correct,* you might think. That was precisely the teacher's point—to teach her students a lesson in prejudice.

The next day she abruptly switched the privileged group from those with blue eyes to those with brown ones. It quickly became clear that both the privileged and unprivileged students acted out their parts based simply on the messages they were receiving about themselves. And if your third-grade teacher has that much influence on how you see yourself, how much more influence will your parents have?

It's extremely difficult to resist negative messages—both spoken and unspoken—that you're told about yourself as a child by your parents and to keep from incorporating those messages into your private logic. How many of us continue into adulthood asking for permission to do certain things because our parents didn't see us as capable of doing them? How many of us think, *I'm not attractive . . . or really all that smart,* simply because those are the messages we received as we were growing up?

No one should make excuses for the hurt they've caused, because there is no excuse that justifies such action. Clearly your parents are responsible for their actions. But there's also a danger in holding others accountable for their actions without holding yourself accountable for yours. Examining your childhood memories is no excuse to forever wag the finger of blame at your parents. If you live life blaming your parents not only for their actions in the past but also for yours in the present, you remain locked in the past.

143

The question I pose to you then is this: *What are you going to do in your present that will unlock your future?*

The Blame Game

There's a little game we all play from time to time that I call the "blame game." We sometimes blame the weather for our attitude, our sports gear for our poor performance, and traffic for our tardiness when we leave the house late for work. Blame often seems a much easier way to cope with life's disappointments.

> What are you going to do in your present that will unlock your future?

Sure, the blame game can feel immensely satisfying when you're clenching that grudge in your fists. But swinging those fists of blame comes with a steep price—your peace of mind, your integrity, and perhaps even the loss of a relationship. Your parents may need to change, and no one may know that better than you do! Unfortunately, trying to change them—or anyone else for that matter—is a fruitless task. As much as you would like to change others' flaws, the only person you can change is yourself.

I realize that when you've been wounded, you want justice. But do you think yourself capable of doling out that justice fairly? Beware,

As much as you would like to change others' flaws, the only person you can change is yourself.

because that is dangerous, holy ground—and should be left for God alone. Can you avoid the danger of your mixed motives transforming you into the very thing that you hate? Can anyone? Are you trying to even up the scales by giving your parents the silent treatment, a heaping spoonful of your bitterness, or a blast of your anger? I understand the motive behind those actions—I've felt them myself—but do you really want to balance the scales with vengeance?

Holding on to a grudge only keeps you from becoming the person you are made to be. It's like taking a bucket of acid and throwing it into a headwind. It's going to come back at you and burn—and keep on burning. When you play the blame game, you end up the loser.

There is, however, another way.

Forgive and . . . Remember

After hearing again and again that Jesus told his followers to forgive people 70 x 7 (Matthew 18:21-22), I finally pulled out my calculator one day. Unless my calculations are off, that's 490 times—and the highest *I've* ever gotten in practicing forgiveness was 3! If I still have 487 more times to forgive someone

When you play the blame game, *you* end up the loser.

for my grievances against him or her, don't you think Jesus had a pretty good handle on how deep hurt can run and how many times we mess up in our relationships? Many people, of course, will tell you to "forgive and forget," but there's a more realistic, healthy way to handle your pain.

Author and professor of theology and ethics Lewis B. Smedes says, "Forgiving does not erase the bitter past. A healed memory is not a deleted memory. Instead, forgiving what we cannot forget creates a new way to remember. We change the memory of our past into a hope for our future."[2] In other words, even though you've forgiven, you're not going to forget your bitter past, so what will you choose to remember? The hurts you've experienced in your past no doubt form some of your most vivid memories—there's no getting around that. There's no way that you can forget those moments any easier than you can forget your marriage to your spouse or the birth of your children.

Think of those who have really hurt you in one way or another. It's not only difficult to forgive those hurts—it's difficult to forget the people, isn't it? If you believe Jesus' admonition to forgive 70 x 7, it puts into context how long this process can take and how difficult it can be. Forgiving is not saying what happened was okay and it's not excusing it—but it is allowing something new to grow. Any person who has reached a point where they can truly say, "I've forgiven that person," would say that the reward at the end of that journey is well worth it. Being able to say "I forgive you" is so much better than being one of those people in my office years down the road, racked with grief over the death of her mother, who says, "I would pay anything to pick up my mother to take her to lunch. I'd give anything just to have one hour together to clear up the things we've said to each other."

Continuing to take those steps toward forgiveness is like running the rapids on a white-water river. There are moments of white-knuckled terror when it seems you've got the Grim Reaper for a guide, but when you're sitting around the campfire that evening looking back on the experience, it doesn't look so bad. What do you say at the end of the journey? "I was so scared during that middle stretch. I thought that was the end, but now I feel great!" When you're taking positive steps, the fear lessens with time (in spite of how it might feel in the middle).

Your parents may never respond the way you hope to your invitation for a new, healed relationship, but isn't the possibility worth the step? There's something wonderfully freeing when you take that baby step forward and are at least able to verbalize "I forgive you"—even if only by saying it out loud to yourself. When you're able to do that, time will begin to heal your wounds.

Does it mean that all will be perfect in your family now? Absolutely not. Just because you forgive someone doesn't mean there will be no consequences in your relationship. You may continue to struggle with hurtful feelings toward your parents for a long time. You may not want to be relationally close to your mother, your father, or both of them.

146

Let me add here that if the relational patterns are toxic enough, it may not even be healthy for you and your parents to live in the same town for a while. If one or both of your parents relate to you, your spouse, or your kids in abusive ways or struggle with alcohol or drug abuse, that can create a toxic environment for your family. What happens when Grandpa and Grandma want to take the kids for the weekend, but Grandpa can't stay sober? Do you really want him driving your little Megan and Melissa to the zoo? Also, if you're a parent who works in a local family business under a controlling father, mother, or other family member, you too may need that physical separation to help break those unhealthy patterns of relating to one another.

As you carefully consider each step, realize that it may be hard. But even if it's a baby step, it's worth taking.

Smoothing over Your Feelings?!

If you were in an automobile accident and were taken to the emergency room, you wouldn't think much of a doctor who enters your examination room, sees blood running down your head, and says to the attending nurse, "Wrap a bandage around her head. When the bleeding stops, send her on her way. Oh," he adds, turning to you, "if you have any further questions, just bottle them up inside."

Not that impressive, huh? Sure, that may cover up your symptoms for a while, but what happens when you start having dizzy spells and blurred vision because of your concussion? No, you want someone willing to take time to listen to how your accident happened, diagnose your injuries precisely, and treat the problem, not just its symptoms.

As obvious as that sounds, I meet so many people when I travel around the country who, when it comes to forgiveness, treat only the symptoms of their wounded relationships, tossing on a flimsy bandage to cover the bleeding without first taking time to assess the problem. They endure treatment from friends and family members time and time again that no human being, let alone a dog, should, and then they brush it aside by saying such things as "Oh, that's just how she is," when that's precisely how she shouldn't be. Some justify their response by pointing to the Bible's admonition to forgive one another, but forgiveness isn't a holy carpet under which all conflicts are swept. Smoothing over your feelings when you've been hurt without adequately assessing the damage and confronting it can make for infected relationships ahead.

I often joke about people sharing "their feelings"—getting cozy with the innermost thoughts of their hearts and telling bedtime stories to their inner child—that sort of thing. But this is no time to joke. It's a time to understand how you've been hurt and what you feel about that hurt. It's especially important to face the truth about how you feel if you are a pleaser or martyr who regularly throws bandages on your wounds to cover the pain others have caused. You might add more and more layers of bandages until you look like a mummy!

Stripping off those layers of excuses and rationalizations is the only way to get healthy. Face the fact that the reason you gained forty pounds may have something to do with your father's physical abuse—perhaps you wanted to make yourself unsightly to push others away. Or perhaps you stay away from crowds because you can't bring yourself to risk being hurt again by new friendships.

Do yourself a favor—tell yourself the truth about your life, because if you smooth over your feelings today, you only make life rougher for yourself tomorrow. Taking your feelings into consideration and facing the truth head-on today, however, will make for smoother roads tomorrow.

Ready for a Shock?

I'm convinced that most of us would probably be happier if we had been the product of the second immaculate conception. Do you think I'm wrong? Stop for a moment and think about your parents having sex.

Yikes—on second thought, maybe not!

Instead of allowing Dad and Mom license to be human, we tend to think of our parents as some kind of alien species, only partly human. Mom existed to make you hot meals, pack your lunch for school, and give you hugs when you scraped your knee. She isn't a lover to anybody and certainly doesn't know what the word *orgasm* means. Dad isn't any better—you probably see him as the only elder in your church who has never had an erection. They may have gotten pregnant during a kiss years back, but that's as much as we're willing to admit. We fabricate our parents like Barbie and Ken dolls, molding them into impossible proportions and dressing them up in our fantasies of who we want them to be—no sex allowed!—not who they really are.

Do yourself a favor— tell yourself the truth about your life.

But as I mentioned earlier in the book, sharing childhood memories with the rest of your family will help fill in a more realistic picture of your parents. If you have siblings, the chances are good that at some time or another you've heard one of them comment about one or both of your parents and you thought, *No, they'd never do that,* because you protect your image of them in your mind.

But, as much as you'd like to believe otherwise, your imagination

148

can't change other people. It doesn't do you much good to walk around for years saying to yourself, "I wish my parents were different." Sure, you may wish they were more like what you imagine them to be—but unfortunately they're not. You could write them off, but the truth is that we all need to be forgiven. You need to be forgiven for the hurts you've caused. I certainly need to be forgiven for the hurts I've caused. Because no one is perfect, we all desperately need forgiveness. By forgiving others you allow them to be human, and in doing so it makes you more aware of how human you really are. Think of all the people you've judged because of their behavior. Isn't it true that some of them behave in very similar ways to you? There isn't a person on the face of this earth who doesn't need grace.

It's unusual to see portraits of that kind of gracious love in our daily lives. When you find them, they really stand out. I recently heard about a neat nonprofit group, Mission Media, in Boise, Idaho, that one day gave out free gas to single moms and dads—no strings attached. People lined up at 5:00 a.m., and that group pumped over $11,000 worth of gas to local single parents. Another day they announced through the mayor's office that if you had an unpaid traffic ticket, you could bring it downtown during certain hours and they would pay it for you. One person walked in with twenty tickets and said, "I have these twenty tickets—I know it's a lot—but if you'd just pay ten, I'd be so grateful."

> We all desperately need forgiveness.

"We'd like to pay all twenty," Executive Director Michael Boerner responded. "Because that's what grace is all about."

If you're looking for a picture of grace, that's a pretty good one. If you're going to succeed in a relationship with your parents, your siblings, or your spouse, you must understand the term *graceful love*. I like that term because it seems to me that you can't have one word without the other. How can you possibly love someone without also offering grace? How can you be gracious without love? Grace is filled with love, and love is full of grace.

Graceful love is especially important when it comes to relating to your parents, because usually the people who hurt you the most are the people closest to you, not strangers. Hurt is a bit easier to shake off when it comes from a stranger. But when a family member or friend has caused it—your mother, father, sister, brother, close friend, grandparent, uncle, or aunt—your pain is intensified by the very nature of your intimate relationship.

Like you, they're imperfect. Yes, they are people who perhaps have done worse things than you have. But people, like you, who need grace simply because they're human.

Are you willing to show them graceful love—that very thing you need yourself?

The Grudge That Stole Christmas

Imagine that every year you and your extended family gather at your parents' house between Christmas and New Year's Day. When the annual reunion was first suggested, the vision was for a scene out of a Norman Rockwell painting. Unfortunately, the reality is closer to a pro-wrestling showdown between your father and your sister's husband. By the time New Year's Day finally rolls around, everyone leaves the house muttering about never wanting to show up for *that* again. As hard as you all try, it's never a very *Merry* Christmas or *Happy* New Year, yet somehow you and your sister were able to coax everyone back again next year for another try.

I don't need to tell you that every family is unique, because I'm sure you could tell me a story that's never been told, a story about your own family growing up. Every family has its own distinct ways of communicating, its own ways of coping with life, and its own shared values. But your family's unique ways also create difficult patterns to break out of. Therefore, when you find that you need to make changes from those family patterns, it's important that you have a game plan. Otherwise being around family can sometimes feel like standing on a slippery slope as you slide back toward those patterns that you are so practiced in but want so much to be free of.

When talking with your parents or other relatives about changing family patterns, recognize that you're all adults. Each one of you is accountable for your own life, so you don't have to all feel or think the same way. You might say something such as "Looking at what's transpired the past two years, I think all of us would admit that we wish our holiday would have happened differently. We probably all wish we wouldn't have said some of the things we did. I have some ideas that I'd like to propose, but first I'd like to hear your ideas, because I sure don't know all the answers. What I do know is this—that I love you and want to always be respectful of you. I want us to be able to get along and to enjoy spending good times together."

You'll need to set some boundaries to keep the past from being repeated. To handle a situation like the one above, you might say, "We certainly appreciate the invitation to stay at your house and the financial advantages of not having to pay for a hotel. But I think it would help for us to get a hotel room this year." I don't doubt that taking a step like that could prove challenging, but it sure beats the

> It isn't enough to simply remember the past. You have to do something about it.

fallout if you don't! (If you're interested in more information on handling a situation such as this one, David Augsburger's book *Caring Enough to Confront* is one I highly recommend.)

You've heard the saying "those who don't remember the past are doomed to repeat it," but it isn't enough to simply remember the past. You have to do something about it, otherwise the past will hijack your future. A game plan helps minimize the possibility of repeating those showdowns—and sets a new course for your relationships.

Here's Your Wake-Up Call

Of all the things that our daughter Hannah inherited from the Leman family genes, "hamburger demolition" ranks high on the list. That came to mind as I was out eating lunch recently with our daughters Hannah and Lauren. As I watched Hannah tear into her hamburger, I couldn't help but remember my father when he was alive, who ate a hamburger as if he were impersonating a wood chipper. As Hannah demolished her burger, I felt a twinge of loss as memories of my father came rushing back. With tears in my eyes and choking out the words, I told Hannah and Lauren that I wished I could still pick him up, take him out, and tell him all that I appreciated about him as he demolished *his* hamburger.

My father and I certainly didn't always have a relationship that open. There was a brief time when, as a teenager, I was convinced I hated him. But around the time I turned 19 I began to see him in a different light. It took me a while to forgive him for some of his flaws, but over the years we became extremely close so that when he died, there weren't two people closer than John and Kevin Leman.

Wherever you are curled up with this book—it might be raining outside; it might be snowing; it might be an overcast fall day in Seattle, or a blustery winter day in Chicago—whatever the weather, this is a great day. You're never going to live this day again, so seize all it has to offer, including the opportunity to take a baby step forward toward reconciliation with your parents.

> You're never going to live this day again, so seize all it has to offer!

If I had waited to mend my relationship with my father, we never would have had the relationship that we eventually did. When he was dying of lung cancer, the doctor told us that about every five months his tumor was doubling in size, so we knew the approximate time frame for his death. But that isn't usually the case. I can't tell you how many people I've talked with who have regretted not mending a relationship with their parents. Over my years of counseling, I'd regularly see a grief-stricken person whose parent had suddenly died shuffle into my office. Sure, it would be helpful if each of us received a wake-up phone call before our parents died: "Hey, by the way, a week from next Tuesday your mom is going to die. Better say the things you've always wanted to say." Unfortunately, most of us never get that kind of call.

But what if that call did come? What if it came a week before your mother's death? That's certainly not much time to say the things you might need to say. So how about a month—or better yet, a year? Would a few years give you the time to work toward a new relationship?

I'll tell you what. I'll give you that wake-up call now!

One day your mother won't be able to call to give you grief even if she wanted to. One day you'll no longer be able to hear your father's gruff voice. It's inevitable. Why wait until a week before that day, if you even have that kind of warning? In spite of whatever may have happened between you and your parents, do you still see your dad as a treasure? Is your mom a treasure? Is your older sister a treasure, even though she's been a colossal pain to you for years? I know having talked with some of you readers that you have been dealt a rough hand in life, but how are you going to play it? Are you going to avoid your parents the rest of your life, or are you going to own up to the fact that neither one of them is perfect and get on with living your life—not imagining the life you want theirs to be? You can't control your parents' responses, but you can control your own. If you don't think that any of them are treasures, what will your feelings be as you stand next to their coffins? Take a moment, put this book down, and stop to think about that. Yes, right now. All I'm asking is seven seconds. . . .

Those difficult events may be off your life's radar at the moment, but what I love about those questions is that they ask you to skip ahead in your life's story to read the last few pages. What will the final lines of those chapters be in your relationships with your parents?

Actor Gene Hackman Chose Grace

Academy Award–winning actor Gene Hackman, who has appeared in dozens of movies in the past half century, wanted to be an actor even as a young boy growing up in Danville, Illinois. He remembers watching a scene from a Jack Oakie comedy film when he was only five or six years old in which the characters were enjoying a feast of food and wine on an ocean voyage.

"That's my memory," said Hackman. "It seemed like a life."[3]

But that world of movies and oceangoing ships serving banquets was far removed from small-town Danville, where Gene lived by the railroad tracks with his parents in his maternal grandmother's house. His father, Eugene, operated the printing press for the local *Commercial News,* where Eugene's father and brother worked as journalists.

One Saturday morning in 1943, when Gene was 13 years old, he was at a friend's house playing in the yard when he glanced up just as his father was driving by. His father waved, and in that moment of catching each other's eye and seeing his father's parting wave, Gene knew his father was never coming back.[4]

There's no denying the hurt his father caused Gene by walking out of his life. Yet over time, Gene Hackman had a greater deal of empathy for people's mistakes in life, and after confronting his father on leaving the family, he came to no longer see his father as a god. Gene chose the way of grace.

"It was silly of me to expect him to change or to understand what he had done," Hackman said. "So I decided I wasn't obliged to be angry anymore, and I feel very good that we were able to spend time together during the five years before he died."[5]

I think he's right on the money, and that the more you mature, the more you realize that we're all flawed and in need of grace.

"No, I wasn't bitter," Hackman said while discussing the incident during an interview on *Larry King Live.* "Disappointed, certainly.

Hurt. I don't think I was ever bitter. I loved him. I loved him right to the end."

"How much of that life experience goes into a role?" King asked to follow up.

"Well, I think everything," said Hackman. "I think when you decide to do a role as an actor, you—if you're honest with yourself, you choose all those things, both the good and the bad that's happened to you. And you try to make that come alive."[6]

You know, that's not simply good acting advice; that's good advice for living. Take both the good and the bad that's happened to you—including the good and bad that's happened in your relationship with your parents as Gene Hackman did—and make your future come alive!

CHAPTER 10

The Inside Skinny on Those You Love

Exploring childhood memories can enrich your relationships

After four decades of being married, I'm still trying to figure out how to love Sande as she wants to be loved—not as *I* would want to be loved if I were her. You'd think that after all these years together I'd be better at reading a woman's mind. I certainly know a lot more . . . but I still don't always get it right.

I was reminded of this when I took Sande out to dinner years ago for her birthday. My idea of a great restaurant is a one-fork greasy spoon. But Sande has a lot more class in her little finger than I've ever had in my entire body, so I took her to a five-star restaurant—a "five-forker" as I like to call it—where you nearly have to pass an etiquette class just to make a reservation.

We had a wonderful dinner and as we left the restaurant and headed home, I was feeling pretty proud of myself. I knew I had hit the bull's-eye that evening because Sande put her arm in mine as we walked up our sidewalk, snuggled close, and said, "Leemie, I just want you to know that this evening was perfect." Then she added, "I'm absolutely exhausted."

Now, there's no *Berlitz Guide to Speaking Womanese,* but I've learned over the years to decipher this kind of Sande-speak. What she was saying was that she was too pooped to whoop, that Mr. Happy was not going to be happy . . . at least not that night.

"But I really enjoyed this," she added with a satisfied glow. "I can't think of a better way to have celebrated my birthday."

In fact, I had thought of a better way to celebrate her birthday—or should I say what I thought was a better way. No sex that evening was the least of my concerns! Hidden behind our front door was an intimate gathering of literally dozens of Sande's closest friends and family members waiting to scream at the top of their lungs, "Surprise!"

You see, as the baby of the family I love surprises. In fact, I crave surprises. If you're ever looking for an excuse to throw me a party, don't wait for my birthday. Throw me a party celebrating a new dental filling or a great parallel parking job. Just surprise me . . . the sky's the limit!

Sometimes, however, I forget that not everyone sees life the way I do. Sande, for example, is a classic firstborn who likes order. She likes the predictable. *Surprise* is definitely not her middle name.

Just as we opened the front door, someone hiding inside flipped on the lights, and everyone yelled, "Surprise!"

What did the birthday girl do? She put her hands over her face and began to cry.

That was my first clue that perhaps my brilliant plan wasn't all I'd imagined it would be. But as the champion of the evening, handling her husband's curveball with grace, Sande rose to the occasion and pretended her tears were tears of joy, covering her true emotions from everyone except me.

How was it that I had so thoroughly missed seeing the world through my wife's eyes? After all these years I should have known that Sande doesn't like to be caught by surprise—after all, I wrote *The Birth Order Book* and know that firstborns generally don't like surprises! Sure, I hit a home run with our dinner plans, but I completely struck out with the surprise party. By any stretch of the imagination, batting one for two—a full .500!—ought to have put me in the Hall of Fame. Unfortunately, in marriage it puts you in the doghouse for a couple of days.

Thankfully, my dear wife extends to me buckets full of mercy and grace. She's certainly experienced at it! And I learned something too—the best-laid plans can be blown sky-high if you don't think them through to their "real conclusion," based on that person's personality.

The lesson I learned all over again is one I'd like to look at in these next few chapters—that not only is it important to acknowledge how your memories form your private logic and lifestyle themes. It's also important to use those techniques in your relationships, in raising your children (or nieces, nephews, or grandchildren), and in your work. Because if you consider others' memories and life themes, you'll be able to begin seeing life through their eyes, too.

And that's when relationships can really sing!

Do You See What They See?

Really seeing life through another person's eyes—what she thinks when she says something to a friend that she didn't intend or how he feels when he fails at work—can be difficult at times, if not downright impossible. It's so much easier to act out of your own private logic, which makes all the sense in the world (at least in your world). Others' private logic often feels, well . . . illogical.

> Others' private logic often feels, well . . . illogical.

Have you ever put on someone else's eyeglasses by mistake or simply for fun? Unless you have precisely the same prescription, the walls suddenly look like cotton batting, people look like aliens in a science-fiction movie, and you'll soon find yourself with a headache. But if you think seeing through someone else's eyeglasses is difficult, try seeing the world through someone else's private logic.

That takes a vigilantly other-centered person. For those of you who are married, it requires setting aside your own agendas and being a

159

lifelong student of your spouse, constantly asking yourself, *What makes him tick?* or *What motivates her to do the things that she does?*

One of the best ways to learn to see through a loved one's eyes is to listen—really listen—to his or her childhood memories and learn the lifestyle themes and private logic of that person.

For those of you who are dating and trying to figure out whether this is "the one," what a gold mine! You can learn all kinds of things about your date that many people don't learn until years into marriage, insights that can mean the difference between a long, hard road twisting ahead of you and a convertible ride together down the straightaway with the top pulled back and the wind in your hair.

Finally, for those of you who simply want to know your friends more deeply, discussing childhood memories is an easy way to get the inside scoop, whether you've known that person for forty minutes or forty years. Whatever relationship you want to nurture, take time to understand that other person's lifestyle themes—in other words, their "theme park."

Exploring Another Person's Theme Park

Disney World has thrilling rides, enough ice cream and cotton candy to feed a battalion of ankle-biters, and smiley, happy Disney characters skipping around Main Street. After all, it's the "happiest place on earth." But though you may love Disney World, would you choose to live there day in and day out?

> Though you may love Disney World, would you choose to live there day in and day out?

I ask that question because when you marry, you'll be visiting your spouse's theme park every day of your life whether you feel like riding the rides or not. Even if you're adept at handling the ups and downs of life, riding that roller coaster 24/7 can test your perseverance. Even the "happiest place on earth" has its rainy days and gets old after a while. On the other hand, if you are able to find someone whose private logic is closer to Winnie the Pooh's than Eeyore's, you'll probably be skipping down Main Street yourself, whistling a happy tune.

Why do you get an MRI when your knee is throbbing with searing pain? You do it to get a priceless glimpse of what's inside. Likewise, listening to your spouse's or date's childhood memories is an excellent way to get a comprehensive look at the way they see life. Anybody can do it simply by sitting down over a cup of coffee and telling stories together. That's a lot more fun than any diagnostic test I can think of.

Take time to visit that other person's theme park as you explore the questions below, because you'll find a vast difference between seeing someone on the outside and seeing that person from the inside out.

- What was the happiest day of your life as a child? Why?
- What was the most difficult moment you faced? Why?
- What were two or three of your biggest disappointments as a kid?
- If you could relive a cherished childhood experience, what would it be? Why?
- What was your first experience with someone close to you dying? How did you feel?
- What memory encapsulates your biggest surprise growing up? Why?
- If there's a memory you could wipe from your childhood memory bank, what would it be?
- When you recall warm feelings from your childhood, what experiences come to mind?
- Do you have any memories that are simply brief snapshots—a falling snowflake, the roar of ocean waves, or a night sky filled with stars? You may not know what its significance is, but what feelings did you attach to those impressions?

Listen for "Aha!" Moments

In chapter 3, we talked about how your psyche takes mental photos with the "aha!" camera as your early childhood experiences match your private logic. I think you'll find that as you listen to your spouse or date share childhood memories and consider those stories for their private logic and lifestyle themes, you too will have some "aha!" moments. You may listen to your wife talk about a childhood memory of being embarrassed in front of her third-grade class and think, *Oh,* that's *why she's so sensitive about that.* Or you may hear your husband talk about his memory of being interrogated by his father on why he put the hammer on the garage workbench precisely where he did and think to yourself, That's *why I've learned never to ask him the question, why?*

Listen carefully for those "aha!" moments, because they will give you invaluable keys to understanding how the other person sees life. As you listen to your spouse, date, or friend tell of childhood memories, you might want to ask what those memories mean to that person. Then reflect later on the following questions yourself:

- Does the private logic behind her memories impede your relationship in any way? What about the private logic behind your memories? Are the ways you both see the world on a collision course for inevitable conflict?

- As you listen to his memories and discern his private logic and lifestyle themes, is there a possibility that both of you are paying for the less-than-satisfactory job his parents did in raising him? If so, what could you do to anticipate the responses of his private logic before they get the best of both of you? What about the responses of your private logic?

Listen carefully, because the more you can gather from those early childhood memories, the more insight you'll gain on that person from the inside out.

How Do People Fit in Memories?

There's a reason you're listening to your childhood memories and there's a reason I encourage you to listen to other people's memories. It all comes down to one important point—*relationships*. Living alongside close friends makes life infinitely richer than living in a solitary box. But not everyone enjoys relating to others. Some people place a higher value on alone time than on time with others. And that can make breaking into their world very difficult.

As you listen to your spouse's or date's memories, then, listen for whether his or her memories deal with people, data, or things. If he is the kind of person who might be an accountant, mechanical engineer, scientist, or one who simply enjoys doing crossword puzzles, you might come across memories that involve solving problems or

> Listen for whether his or her memories deal with people, data, or things.

succeeding academically. Perhaps he remembers playing with an Erector set or watching beetles crawling under a log in the woods. There is nothing wrong with those memories, but if that person has very few or no memories with people in them, I suggest you pay attention to how he or she relates to others today. It may be that he is simply an introspective person, comfortable being by himself, well-adjusted and well-liked by everyone he comes in contact with. But if that person is a social loner, beware, because you probably don't want a hermit who hides out from society—unless, of course, you are a hermit yourself.

Another question to consider as you listen is how important family members are in that person's memories. Are his mother and father distant characters when they appear in his memories or are they an integral part of those memories? That distinction is important because a marriage isn't just between two people. It brings together at least six—you, your spouse, your spouse's parents, and your parents—and he'll bring his attitudes toward his parents into your marriage. (A marriage involves even more than six people if either one of your parents is divorced and remarried, or if you previously divorced.) That doesn't mean people can't change—they certainly can and if he has made great strides to change his private logic from a difficult childhood, that perseverance is a wonderful quality. It should be applauded. However, if all his early childhood memories involving family are negative, ask yourself, *How are his relationships with his family today?*

So when considering others' memories, ask yourself:

- Do his memories involve people? If not, is it apparent by watching his behavior why not? Or has he made great strides to change his private logic?
- What kind of early memories does she have that involve interacting with family members?
- Having listened to his childhood memories, what would you say his private logic and lifestyle themes are?

Also listen carefully to your spouse's, date's, or friend's early childhood memories about the opposite sex. For most people, of course, their father or mother will be the first to come to mind, but what memories emerge involving the opposite sex other than parents? If you're considering your own memories of the opposite sex, contrast how you felt in your memory with how you feel relating to the opposite sex now. In what ways does your private logic in your childhood memories play itself out in your relationships today? You be the "shrink" and assess what you can from those memories to see what they tell you about yourself now.

Here are some good questions to ask yourself:

- Are your first memories of the opposite sex (other than your parents) positive or negative?

- Can you remember the first *positive* memory you have of interacting with the opposite sex? Can you remember your first *negative* memory of interacting with the opposite sex? Why do you think you remember those interactions?

A word of caution. If, after examining your childhood memories involving your family and considering your private logic and lifestyle themes you can't say to yourself, "I really feel loved by those closest to me, my family," and you're beginning to date, beware. Your propensity will be to be drawn like a moth to a flame to people who aren't good for you, who repeat unhealthy patterns you grew up with, who may even treat you terribly, reinforcing any unhealthy views you have of yourself.

Finally, for those of you who are married, you're already living in your spouse's theme park. I hope that hearing your spouse's childhood memories brings you "aha!" moments of greater understanding. Keep pressing in, for your motivation for doing this is to be as emotionally, physically, and spiritually close to your spouse as you can. (Just remember that you, too, have to risk being vulnerable by sharing your own memories with your spouse and letting him or her take an intimate look inside you.) And when you're involved in your next misunderstanding (I assume that's a given), stop for a second. Before you open your mouth to respond, think of both of your lifestyle themes and private logic. Those two unique perspectives will help you understand why you and your loved one are responding the way you are.

Thinking through the why and giving yourself a few minutes to respond can take a lot of the heat out of a battle. It will also take the sting away from many future memories because you're less likely to blurt out your emotions and more likely to weigh each word first.

Yes, it takes time to understand each other through the sharing of your childhood memories. But the results—both short-term and long-term—are worth it!

Help Him Open Up without Closing Him Down

"Dr. Leman," I imagine some of you women are saying, "I would love to talk with the man in my life about his childhood memories, but I just can't imagine him being interested in talking about what his life was like when he was a little boy. I can barely get him to open up about what happened today at work."

Here's a great way to do it. Share a memory about your childhood and don't tell him up front the significance of what childhood memories mean. Then ask him if he remembers an adventure from his childhood. If it helps, prompt him by asking about something you know he's interested in such as "Did you catch many fish when you were really young?", or "So when was the first time you remember going camping?" Then respond to the memory by saying something like "That sounds like a fun time in your life! Tell me more about that."

As you talk, remember the basic tenet of communication: Judgments push you apart, whereas sharing feelings draws you together. Don't ask, "Why did you feel that way?" because questions asked like that come across as judgmental to men and cause them to put up defenses. Simply saying, "Tell me more," however, shows interest on your part. If your man is typical of the male species, he's going to be eager to tell you more about that early childhood memory of catching his first fish or rigging his Cub Scout tent to keep out the rain at 2:00 a.m. You see, men like to talk about the adventures in their lives, their victories and "scar stories," so such stories are a good entry point into a conversation about his childhood. Anytime you get a man who's usually out tinkering in the garage to talk about his early childhood memories, hey, you're getting someplace!

Of course, a man generally doesn't have the same trouble getting the woman in his life to talk about her memories. If you ask a woman what time it is, she'll generally tell you what time it is, as well as what kind of watch she has, where she bought it, and how much she paid for it on sale. Statistically, the average woman uses seven thousand words per day, while the average man uses only two thousand words per day.[1] I heard it jokingly said that the reason for the discrepancy is that women have to repeat everything they say to the men in their lives. Seriously though, all you men reading this have an open door to talk about childhood memories with the women in your life—your sisters, your date, your wife, or your daughters—all you need to do is raise the subject.

> The average woman uses seven thousand words per day, while the average man uses only two thousand words per day.

167

And let me tell you from experience that asking the woman in your life about her childhood memories is a great use of your two thousand words. What you discover about her private logic and lifestyle themes will help you decipher her responses and get to the heart of the matter . . . whether you're talking about matters of the heart or not.

Truth Therapy Is Just What the Doctor Ordered

Relationships bring out the best in us—and the worst in us. I don't mean that negatively. In fact, I believe that intimate friendships stretch us from the inside out, revealing our weak areas. But because you're immersed in the relationship, it can be difficult to recognize the ways you perpetuate patterns of enabling your loved one's weaknesses or hold him or her back from growing. At times you need an outside reference point to help you objectively see yourself and how you're relating. Studying your childhood memories and private logic together as a couple can be just the thing to give you that objectivity.

When Miles and his wife, Jan, came to me for counseling, he was driving her bonkers by taking music gigs in seedy bars. He was working until 2:00 a.m., rubbing shoulders with people who weren't good for him, and coming home smelling like he'd rolled in an ashtray. Miles was extremely talented musically but had run with a rough crowd growing up and struggled to use his musical talent in ways that didn't put him on the fringe of trouble. He came to believe in God later in life but continued to see himself as an outsider socially. As a result, he had a difficult time discerning how best to use the talent he'd been given.

I genuinely enjoyed Miles. He was authentic. He was searching. And he fully admitted it. His wife was very supportive of him and came to every counseling session. Together, the three of us began exploring Miles's childhood memories one by one. Although there was nothing traumatic in his background, his memories shared a common theme. Miles always seemed to be getting in trouble, and that pattern became a lifestyle theme for him. He had learned to see himself in such negative terms that he continued to struggle to use his gifts in a positive way.

As I got to know Miles and Jan, I spotted something else, too. Jan was clearly a perfectionist, and in conversation she often hammered Miles with her extremely high standards without realizing it. Her holier-than-thou attitude ticked him off, though he'd never said anything to her about it. But he always felt like he could never quite measure up to her expectations of him, which perpetuated his negative views of himself.

Both Miles and Jan needed to do a lot of work in identifying their private logic and then seeing how that had formed their individual lifestyle themes. Jan began to realize how much her perfectionist tendencies were shutting Miles down. As she focused on understanding the private logic and lifestyle themes in Miles's childhood memories, she learned to keep her mouth shut, back off, and not only accept him for who he was, but offer him encouragement that combated the lies his private logic was telling him.

And that's exactly what she needed to do. If you are married, part of your job is to help your spouse not beat himself up in those areas where he's weak. If you focus on the positive, you bring balance to your spouse's negative image. It was a tough job for Jan, especially since she was tough not only on Miles but on herself, too. She had to change her own rulebook before she could be supportive of Miles. Both of them realized that identifying their private logic and lifestyle themes was just what the doctor ordered, for it set them free from the relational patterns they were locked in.

What does your relationship need? Are you locked in patterns that you wish you could get out of? Are you finding it hard to see past where you are right now to a different kind of future?

You, too, can be set free. As you begin to understand more about the person God has created you to be, that self-understanding will bring compassion for yourself. It will also bring compassion for your loved ones, who may be struggling to figure out who they are. As you see the truth about yourself reflected back through the understanding of a good friend, you can relax, taking the small steps toward healing and restoration.

It won't happen overnight. You've learned to become the person you are over many years. But just as you learned your undesirable behavior, you can also unlearn that behavior.

In the end, Miles chose to arrange music for their church and got involved in various community plays and musicals. The work was perfectly suited to Miles's talents, the hours were better suited to family life, and he received the much-needed pats on the back that he had longed for as a little boy and never received. As he settled into his new life, he didn't even miss the negative track in his old life because he was satisfied and fulfilled.

As Miles relaxed in his new lifestyle and became less "wild," Jan became less dictatorial and perfectionistic. Not only was she now getting a good night's sleep, she was relieved his talents were being put to good use and that Miles felt happy about his contribution to the community. Miles and Jan also discovered that, in spite of their differences, they were a really good match. They had just needed to fine-tune their relationship!

After looking at your own childhood memories and the memories of your spouse, date, or friend, you may find yourself concluding that you really do balance each other in spite of your differences. Perhaps this chapter has helped you see that you need your loved one's strengths more than you realized.

Did you know that couples tend to fill voids in each other's lives? If you're the life of every party, you may have matched up with the strong, silent type. If you are introspective, chances are good that you married someone who is quite comfortable using up the minutes on your cell-phone plan. There is truth to the old adage that "opposites attract."

Couples tend to fill voids in each other's lives.

Why were you attracted to your loved one in the first place? Because he was exactly like you? Because she was good at all the same things you are? Probably not! You grew to love that person because he or she was so different and intriguing that you were captivated enough you wanted to spend a lifetime together.

Many couples make good teams in large part because they balance each other. One wife may help the couple live in the moment, while her husband has a mind for helping them plan ahead. Another wife's organizational skills may give her social-butterfly husband a place to land. In turn, his social abilities help her fly too. The combinations, like the matchups themselves, are infinite. You really do need others—and others need you. God's observation that it was not good for us to be alone[2] was right on.

So much treasure is hidden in your memories that it is well worth the digging. Yes, sometimes it may be painful. You may get scraped-up knuckles or sore knees from digging around in the dirt. But understanding your childhood memories will not only explain your actions and reactions in the present, it will also help redirect your actions and reactions in the future. It can affect you, your spouse or spouse-to-be, your children or children-to-be, your friends, your distant relatives—anyone you come into contact with.

The effect is more far-reaching that you could ever dream!

171

CHAPTER II

Zap 'em with a Psychological X-ray (Your Kids Will Probably Even Enjoy It!)

Is your child heading in the right direction?
How to know for sure.

At some time or another all parents look at their children and think, *If only I could get into my kids' heads.* You may try talking with your son as he's staring out the SUV window after striking out in the bottom of the ninth inning of his Little League baseball game. But for all your coaxing, you may only end up striking out yourself. You may try asking your daughter if she's okay as she's picking through dinner after the first day of a new school year but receive little more than a deflated "yeah."

What in the World Is Going through Their Minds?

You know your children better than anyone, but could you articulate your child's private logic? Can you tell me in a few sentences how she sees the world and her place in it? Would you like to know what kind of pathway is being built in his personality or even what direction he might be taking in life?

You can put childhood memories to excellent use in helping raise the kids in your life, whether you're a mother, father, grandparent, aunt, or uncle. Sharing childhood memories together as a family is a great way to take a psychological X-ray of your child's private logic, getting inside her head and seeing life through her eyes. Reflecting on your children's early memories as well as your own will help you understand who your children really are deep down inside and how your own background influences the way you parent them. It will give you wonderful insight into how to raise them in a way that best suits them. And you'll learn how to nurture a positive environment in your family as you make memories together both now and in the future.

There's no better place to start than by casually talking about childhood memories as you're going about your daily activities. Bringing up childhood memories with your kids shouldn't involve a heavy talk. In fact, it will work much better if it doesn't. Sometime during a lull in conversation at the dinner table or as you're driving to the grocery store, mention a childhood memory of yours very matter-of-factly. You might say, "You know, I was just thinking about something that happened when I was a kid." Then briefly tell your memory and—here's the kicker—ask your kids why they think you remember what you remember.

174

> We don't give our kids the credit they deserve, but they're smart little buzzards. They know you better than you may realize.

Sometimes we don't give our kids the credit they deserve, but they're smart little buzzards. They know you better than you may realize, and you may be surprised to find that, given the opportunity, they'll probably come up with the theme of this book by themselves—that your early childhood memories hold the key to how you see life. As your kids figure this out, they'll enjoy playing the role of Mom's and Dad's shrink. And in the process, they'll grow more open and excited about talking about what they remember themselves.

You might ask them, "What do you remember growing up?" Your little boy or girl may only be five or six years old—barely off the training wheels on her bike—but she'll probably rise to the occasion to talk about what it was like way back when she was a kid. Whether your child is a teenager ready to fly the coop or a first grader still clinging to the nest, you're bound to gain insight into who they are and how they see life as you listen to their memories.

Remember, as your kids share their stories, they may remember similar events but have very different interpretations. In fact, they may say in response to a brother's or sister's memory, "*That's* not the way it happened!" Before the debate comes to blows, point out that both of their perspectives could be correct—that different people see the same event in different ways because we're all unique people.

On behalf of all the children, however, please don't force this conversation, calling a family meeting and sitting your children around the table. There's nothing worse than turning a great meal together or a commute home from school into an inescapable Psych 101 class with Dad and Mom Freud. This isn't a session on the counseling-office couch, nor is it a psychological interrogation under the dining-room lights.

So treat it casually, and I think you'll find that your kids will respond not only with interest but with enthusiasm.

Creating Positive Memories

As you listen to your kids' memories, you may be surprised. What you think they may say are highlights won't be. For example, I can almost guarantee that the events most impressed on their psyches don't include the four-day, five-night family trip to Disney World two years ago that you spent thousands of dollars on.

When you're driving to Disney World, what are your kids doing? They're shuffling through their playlists on their iPods, they're attempting to reach level 11 on their Game Boy games, they're product-testing the strength of their seat belts, and their bladders are competing in the relay event of the Rest Stop Olympics. Your husband is sitting next

175

to you in the passenger seat snoring, with drool dribbling down the corner of his mouth. You're drinking your fifth cup of tepid gas-station coffee on your way to Florida, while your own bladder is going for the gold.

This is family closeness?

Sure, you may be in close proximity, but you're not necessarily doing anything together. Even when you reach Disney World, your older kids want to ride the roller coasters, your little kids want to spin around in the teacups, and, truth be told, you'd prefer to simply lie around next to the pool all day.

While your kids no doubt enjoyed that trip—and will certainly say so if asked—do you know what your daughter is much more likely to remember? She'll probably recall the evening she was horrified to crash the hard drive on your computer. You may have forgotten that evening, but she remembers. She was trying to delete an old draft of her social studies current-events paper and instead she irretrievably trashed the computer's entire operating system.

Whoops.

But do you know what she remembers most vividly? Your response . . . you putting your arm around her and telling her that you loved her no matter what. You did give her "the look," and she remembers how much she deserved that look.

> Your child will never forget how you handled that moment.

But she'll never forget how you handled that moment. She felt bad enough, but you didn't make her feel worse, and that made her feel loved unconditionally.

You see, creating positive memories for your children is more about the time you take with them, the priority you place on your relationship, and the love you show them than any gift you might give them at Christmas or any vacation you might take as a family.

In truth, you communicate by everything you do. It takes time and love—not money and activity—to create positive memories.

Like Father, Like Son

I shared a memory at the beginning of this book in which the activist Martin Luther King Jr. recalled his father walking out of an Atlanta shoe store when they were told they had to wait in the back until the white customers had been served. It had a profound effect on his son, who then passed on the lesson by his actions to *his* son, as you can see in Martin Luther King III's childhood memory:

177

> Until his father was called "a jailbird," King [Martin Luther King III], whose father was assassinated when he was 10 years old, thought all adults were regularly arrested and put in jail.
>
> "I came home crying profusely," he says of the day a schoolmate taunted him. "I had been crying all afternoon and my mother said: 'You must understand that your father is going to jail to make this world a better place for all of God's children.' After I heard that, I went back to school the next day with a lot of joy and pride. Not arrogance, but I was proud of the fact that he was going to jail and trying to make a difference in that way."[1]

It's profound, isn't it, how much Martin Luther King Sr. communicated to his son by walking out of that Atlanta shoe store? He didn't have to say a word to show that *all* people are to be treated with respect, that the behavior they received was unacceptable, and that neither of them had to put up with it. Decades later, Martin Luther King Jr. followed his father's example by standing up for what was true and showing by his actions that going to jail for what was right was "normal" behavior. And *his* son got the message loud and clear too.

Whether by words, actions, or both, you communicate through everything you do.

Whether by words, actions, or both, you communicate through everything you do. You communicate the importance of honesty to your children by whether or not you give the grocery store checkout cashier the five dollars he overpaid you in change. You communicate to them your values by how you respond when they scrape their bike handlebars down the side of your new car. Whether your children go to public school or private school, whether they're tutored by you at home or whether they attend a local schooling co-op, you are a homeschooling parent simply by the way you live out your values and beliefs before your children. Even more important than trying to create a positive memory in your child's life through certain experiences is living a positive, memorable life before them. That, dear parent, is the kind of environment that will create positive memories in your children—though it certainly takes setting boundaries in your family to make it happen.

178

Give Your Family Lots of Vitamin N

When your child signs up for soccer, there are all kinds of costs. There's the $60 registration fee for the season. There are the shin guards, cleats, and soccer clothes to buy at the local sporting goods store. But there's also another cost that you aren't billed for right away, one that you will pay for over the months to come—time away from the family.

> Even more important than trying to create a positive memory in your child's life through certain experiences is living a positive, memorable life.

When one of your children plays soccer, everybody is in soccer. Little brother and sister are in soccer. Your spouse is in soccer. You are in soccer. The dog and his very important ball time and evening walk are in soccer. Dinnertime is in soccer. In short, your entire family is in soccer, so I urge you to count the cost well before family life reaches the chaotic frenzy of a World Cup final.

Don't get me wrong. I'm not saying that soccer or baseball or football is a bad activity. Our daughter Hannah loved playing volleyball in high school, and Sande and I thoroughly enjoyed watching her games. But don't expect to have everyone scattered around the city within a twenty-mile radius every day of the week for each of your children's two to three activities and still have a cohesive family. Instead, give yourself and your family what I call Vitamin N—the practice of saying no to too many activities. It may be a difficult line to draw, but it's not a hard word to say.

179

Go ahead, try it. Say n-o.

There, that wasn't so bad, was it? I recommend that you pleasers even try practicing it out loud until you feel comfortable saying it at a moment's notice. Stand in front of the bathroom mirror and turn on the fan so no one will hear you or practice during your morning shower. Rehearse saying such things as "As much as I really would like to, I can't." Or "You know, I'll have to get back to you on that," in order to get yourself out of the immediate situation so you can gather strength to later say, "No." Or there's the straightforward approach: "No, I'm sorry." Getting used to saying no will help when you need to draw those lines to protect unscheduled time at home, but everything within your private logic is telling you to mouth the word yes.

Go ahead, try it. Say *n-o*.

Your kids will take their cues from you, so Vitamin N starts with you drawing some boundaries. It doesn't do you any good to tell your daughter, "Beatrice, you need to eat your veggies. I know Mom and Dad don't do it, but do what we say, not what we do." Likewise, if you tell your kids they can't join too many activities, but you serve on the PTA committee, sing in the church choir, and colead a Bible study with your husband, who serves on two boards and coaches both of your kids' T-ball teams, who's kidding whom? If you don't take Vitamin N yourself, your kids won't escape the "activity trap" any better than you are.

A good principle to follow to help encourage Vitamin N and nurture positive childhood memories in your kids is that no one member of the family is more important than the whole. With the majority of mothers today not only bringing home the bacon but also frying it, families have only so much time. That's why I recommend a maximum of one activity per child per term to maintain family cohesiveness.

You may protest by saying, "Dr. Leman, you don't know our son. He is a very gifted athlete and has great potential to make it big."

I'm sure that he and half a million others like him around the country will "enjoy" competing for the spots on the regional select teams . . . which will enable him to compete for the handful of college spots five years down the road . . . which over the following four years will give him a long shot at the few pro spots. If that doesn't work out, all you've wasted is the majority of his childhood and any chance at teaching him proper perspective in life. No big deal. If you want your son to live, breathe, and eat football, he may even make it to the pros (though the odds of that happening are probably less than being hit by lightning)—but what kind of a family will you have?

You see, when you say yes to one activity, you always say no to something else. Always. You might not know what you're saying no to, but you always cut out something you could be doing. I'd argue that what you're cutting out is time together at home as a family. If there's no downtime in your schedule, a lot of people are going to pay for that. Most parents don't want their kids left behind, but left behind in *what?* Look around at other families driving hundreds of miles across the state every weekend for a ninety-minute soccer game. Do you really want your kids to be like other kids? That's the life many have chosen, but I'm telling you that you don't have to live it. More activities do not make for better, more well-adjusted children. In fact, I'd argue that too many activities make for less well-adjusted children. Sure, your son may know how to score goals like no one's business, but is that his only goal in life? Is kicking a ball well his primary value? And what happens when he misses that clutch, last-minute shot on goal? What will his private logic tell him about himself then?

How do you replace the activity trap to help create positive early childhood memories for your kids, when one's cocooning himself in his room playing an Xbox game online, another's in her room IMing her friends on the computer, and another is stretched out on the living room couch watching Cartoon Network reruns?

I have some ideas.

Level the Playing Field

Your family may live under one roof, but at times it may seem that everyone wants to do his or her own thing. Because each person has a different personality, abilities, and interests, it helps from time to time to level that playing field, so to speak, since the family that works and plays together, stays together.

In the Leman household, one of our favorite things is spontaneous nights together. Not scheduled, pen-it-on-the-calendar family nights, which to me feel like force-fed family fun. I'm not going to stand up at dinnertime, tap my fork on my milk glass, and say, "Now hear this; now hear this! On Friday night, I want everyone to drop what you're doing for some scheduled fun. This is our regular, appointed night to have lots and lots of fun. And if you don't all enjoy yourselves, your mother and I will be very disappointed."

Can your family really have a good time within those parameters? Don't you find that some of the most fun, the most creative, the most bonding times together as a family are unplanned? Of course, you all have to be around the home for that kind of spontaneity to happen— which is why Vitamin N is so important—so make sure you leave time for creativity. The next time you see the family lounging around the living room, come up with something like "Hey, let's make home-made pizzas using any ingredients you can find around the kitchen. Anything. See how creative each of you can get. Then let's pop some popcorn in the living room with the air popper's top off. Let's make a popcorn volcano!" Or run with one of your kid's ideas. (It's a tough world out there competing for your family's attention, so if you'd like more information on how to go about refocusing family life back to, well, your family, see my book *Home Court Advantage*.)

Bonding family activities often work simply because they level the family's playing field—anybody can get involved from your four-year-old daughter to your son home from college for the weekend. If your family has any inclination to be outdoors, camping is a great way to create memories together. When you get away from it all, you don't have the distractions of home pulling you in half a dozen directions, and much of the fun is in watching Mom trying to cook over a campstove and Dad wrestling with the tent, or the new challenge of starting a campfire or catching a fish. Even better is looking back on the experience around the campfire that evening, enjoying a laugh together at Mom shrieking at the garter snake by the woodpile and the tent collapsing on Dad!

The principle of the level playing field also applies when you're working on projects around the house. If you're adding a deck onto your home, what's healthier than having everybody pitch in? If your 12-year-old son is into drafting, have him help with the design and calculations. Ask your three-year-old daughter to help pick out flowers for pots on the deck. The wise parent asks her child, "What do you think we ought to do?" because that gives your child a perfect opportunity to see that she belongs to the family, that her ideas are appreciated, and that she is able to contribute in meaningful ways.

That way everyone contributes—young and old alike—whether your family is at work or play.

Clue into Your Own Parenting Challenges

After you've taken that psychological X-ray of your children to assess their private logic, it's also a good idea to consider your own memories to identify areas in your parenting style that might present challenges.

Imagine this scenario. Only-born, British-raised Constance marries Antonio, a charming Italian who is the fourth of five boys. Now Antonio is probably going to be used to chaos, conflict, and solving interpersonal problems, whereas Constance may be much more used to... well... constants. Her early childhood memories may include playing by herself in her room and watching rain pour down outside, while she felt peaceful and sheltered inside. Antonio's memories, on the other hand, may include the satisfaction of wrestling a toy away from his younger brother and getting away with it.

> The wise parent asks her child, "What do *you* think we ought to do?" because that gives your child a perfect chance to see that she belongs to the family, that her ideas are appreciated, and that she is able to contribute in meaningful ways.

It's not difficult to realize that Constance may be a bit shell-shocked when it comes to figuring out how the two of them are going to solve the inevitable conflicts that come with marriage. Then, when Constance feels she has the slightest clue how to handle conflict in their marriage and their own kids begin wrestling for toys, she might not know what in the world to do. She'll be thinking, *Why can't they get along?* In fact, that will probably become a mantra running through her head. Why can't they just get along?! After all, she got along just fine with all the adults around her as she was growing up—her parents, her grandparents, and her parents' friends who came over and praised her on how well behaved she was during British teatime.

Look at your own childhood memories, private logic, and lifestyle themes for clues to the challenges you might face in parenting. If you're an only-born child like Constance, your need for harmony and order might drive the way you see the world. Likewise, if you were a firstborn child, you may like being in control because you exercised some degree of control over your younger siblings. Both the only-born and the firstborn child, therefore, might need to consciously consider relaxing a bit when it comes to both marriage and parenting to push against that private logic of unreasonable harmony and control.

At the other end of the spectrum, you babies of the family will be much more comfortable with the buzz of activity that Antonio's family enjoyed, so your task might be to push against your tolerance for chaos and be more disciplined. Middleborn children, accustomed to compromise and being peacemakers and thus a bit more difficult to pin down, might need to work on facing conflict head-on and taking action, depending on what balance needs to be brought to your private logic.

Because everyone's private logic is unique, birth order won't tell the whole story about the challenges you might face in parenting. So take a close look at your childhood memories and private logic to see what you might be facing. If there's a need for change in your family and the way you parent, it has to start with you. I suggest you address it head-on with your children by beginning with an apology for not doing things the way you wish you would have. That apology will probably catch your child completely off guard and make him much more open to listening. The change in your parenting approach may cause some volatility in the short term, especially if your child is in what I call the "hormone group," the pubescent and adolescent years.

But I believe that if the changes you see are truly needed, the shift will be worth it in the long haul.

Live a Loving Life, and Positive Memories Will Follow

Wherever you and your child are in life, childhood memories are a great way to take that psychological X-ray of your kids as well as examine yourself to identify potential challenging areas in your parenting style. Perhaps you've never considered your child's private logic. Perhaps you've been stampeding along with other families in your neighborhood right into the activity trap. So many of us measure our children by others' standards, looking to see whether they're at the top of their football game or the top of their class.

In the end, what standard matters?

But, in the end, what standard matters? When you stop to think about it, what do you want your kids to be most known for? The fastest time on the track team or the slowest temper? The highest grade in the class or the highest respect of her peers? An Olympic gold medal or a heart of gold? Ah, the long-range view puts a lot of things in perspective, doesn't it?

If you give your children the love and leisurely attention they need, their positive early childhood memories will probably be stored away in their psyches when you least expect it. They'll be stored at a time when what came out of your caring heart—not your pockets—spoke most clearly to them.

185

CHAPTER 12

Are You a Fish out of Water?

Put your memories to work in your work

As I travel around the country, I meet so many people who tell me they're dissatisfied with their work. I can hear in their voices the disappointment, the disillusionment, and the what-ifs:

"I got a job offer a couple of years ago for something I would have loved doing, but I was afraid to take it. My wife and I were just having our third baby. What if I failed? I couldn't take that chance."

"Running an in-home day care is not what I envisioned myself doing when I graduated from college with a BA in journalism."

"I wish I could change careers, because working outdoors is killing me. But I'm now 50, too close to retirement for anybody else to want me."

"I always wanted to be a mother, but that's not all I thought I'd be."

They all hoped their feelings would change as they settled into their positions, but the further along they got, the more stuck they felt. Many appear resigned to keep plodding along in the same rut, whether they're managing a multimillion-dollar corporation, running a home business, or volunteering in their community while the kids are in school.

If This Sounds Familiar, You're Not Alone.

Salma is 29 and just returned to the workplace two years ago after staying home for six years to raise their son, Kiran. Salma and her husband needed the extra money and both were delighted when she secured a well-paying job in the accounting department of a Web-development firm. Salma loves the people she works with and believes strongly in the company, but her position itself weighs on her. There is a lot of desk work, and she is a very social person. Though she works hard, she regularly leaves the computer spreadsheets at her desk for breaks to chat with the receptionists. Interestingly, though, her boss hasn't confronted her about this chatting. On the contrary, she overheard him telling the CEO that whenever clients come in and she happens to be in that front office, her conversation inevitably leaves them much more enthusiastic about doing business with their company.

188

Recently her husband suggested that she talk to her boss about switching jobs within the company, but Salma knows there aren't any positions open. *Isn't that like saying I don't want the job I have?* she worries. *We need the money. Besides, with today's market, I'm lucky just to have this job.*

Would it surprise you if I were to tell you that Salma's childhood memories would probably involve people and that the feelings accompanying those memories are warm ones? Managers would pay plenty for her ability to make those around her feel immediately at home, and I'll bet that she could sell you a monthly subscription for dead rats if she wanted to and leave you feeling like you'd received the deal of a lifetime! Though Salma may be able to bear her accounting job for a while, and though her family may need the money until she can transition to another job, she's clearly a fish out of water. If Salma and her husband are wise, they'll try to eventually get her another job. If her boss is wise and doesn't want to find himself telling a tale about "the one that got away," he'll switch her to a sales or even managerial position before he loses her to another pond.

Because while Salma may be a fish out of water in her accounting job, when she's working directly with people, she's swimming in home waters!

Are You a Fish out of Water?

When I was a boy, the shores of Ellicott Creek near our house in Williamsville, New York, were practically a home away from home for me. If you added up the hours I spent there over the years—winter mornings trapping, fall afternoons exploring the shoreline after school, and summer days fishing—I probably spent more time there than I did in class! I knew more about how to fish, where to fish, and when to fish on Ellicott Creek than I knew about algebra or U.S. history. Ellicott Creek was the only subject a boy like me needed, and I learned from my days there that whenever I hooked a fish, it did everything in its power to return to water. It would flip and flop, clearly out of its element, until it settled down and accepted the sad inevitability.

189

Sounds a lot like many of the people I meet today.

Salma is so social she could carry on a conversation with a friend's photo on her cubicle wall, but what does she do for a living? She sits in a back room in front of a computer screen and toggles back and forth between Excel spreadsheets all day. That sure sounds to me like a fish out of water. Her personality is much better suited to direct contact with clients, and her caliber of people skills is not easily acquired.

I realize that at times you'll find yourself out of water through no choice of your own. You may be faced with severe financial pressures, so rather than kicking back on the living-room couch because you can't find a job that "suits your talents," you wisely flop around in a less-than-desirable position for the time being. Life isn't always the party we'd like it to be. Even fish traveling upriver to spawn must sometimes navigate shallow water to cross gravel bars. I'm sure they're not overly excited about sucking air and exposing themselves to hungry bears, but they do it to complete the job at hand.

Pay attention to your childhood memories and what they reveal about your private logic and lifestyle themes, because they can provide a key to the kinds of work you should be pursuing in life—whether you're considering what major to choose in college (business administration or music performance?), how to contribute to your neighborhood's block party (going door-to-door to invite people or coordinating the food prep?), or which position to apply for in your company for a promotion (human-resources manager or senior-systems analyst?).

The answer may very well be hidden in your childhood memories.

A Perfect Match

Years ago, a publisher in California told me that one of his earliest childhood memories was of directing neighborhood kids from the ground as they built a tree house. "That early childhood memory is very telling," I said to him, "because you're still directing people." There are all sorts of people involved in publishing a book—a lot of people climbing around up in the tree, so to speak—to make it what it is when it reaches your local bookstore. I suppose that if he had played his cards radically differently, he could have turned out to be a tyrannical controller, telling people in no uncertain terms what to do, how to do it, and how they were deviating from his plan. But instead he turned out to be a prime example of what a healthy controller can be, and that childhood memory affirms that he is swimming in precisely the right waters.

Sometimes a childhood memory of yours can provide clues to what you ought to be doing in life or can confirm that you're in the right or wrong work for you. Remember when I was a kid feeling that stirring desire to travel as I heard an airplane whining overhead? Remember years later, as I was standing in the middle of that gymnasium making people laugh? I think both of those memories reveal aspects of my makeup that have become part of my job today—travel and public speaking. Both experiences provided telltale clues pointing out the path I chose to make a living.

But your childhood memories can provide more insight than simply what you might do for a living. They're also helpful in identifying hobbies and activities that nurture you at your core. I recently heard about one young woman's childhood memory from when she was about three or four years old. She recalls the thrill of dancing around the classroom with the rest of the students, twirling long, red ribbons and pushing to overcome her inhibitions until she felt pure enjoyment.

Your childhood memories can provide more insight than simply what you might do for a living—they're also helpful in identifying hobbies and activities that nurture you at your core.

Today she's considering joining a modern dance class after she gives birth to her first child, to help nurture herself during that time when she'll be focusing so much energy on their new baby.

Pay attention to similar memories of yours with strong positive feelings or happy endings, because they can provide clues to what you should be doing in life, whether it's your vocation or leisure activities. Likewise, if you have negative memories or ones with sad endings they can communicate personal weaknesses, areas to grow in, or directions that aren't necessarily putting your best foot forward.

191

How wonderful to enjoy your life's work because you're swimming in the right waters! What if you also knew how to nurture yourself during your downtime by participating in activities that your childhood memories reveal are particularly meaningful and nurturing to you? Who knows? You might even wake up day after day excited to do what lies before you because you're following your own unique design.

Sounds to me like a prescription for a positive mental health and an uplifting outlook on life!

People, Data, or Things?

When I was an assistant dean of students at the University of Arizona, one of the administrators who worked in financial services helping the college kids once said to me, "You know, this would be a great place to work if it weren't for the students."

What a terrible thing to say! Sure, we need people who prefer being glued to their seats, people who enjoy staring at blips on computer screens. I'm profoundly grateful to those in the control tower every time my flight touches down safely on a clear runway here in Tucson. But if your job requires a lot of face-to-face time with people, make sure that you're able to . . . well . . . enjoy facing people. We certainly don't need someone counseling students who would rather be in a private cubicle, just as we don't need air-traffic controllers acting as social butterflies, cracking jokes up in the tower and throwing paper airplanes at one another as a real plane careens onto a crowded runway.

> How wonderful to enjoy your life's work because you're swimming in the right waters!

To get an idea of the general direction for your work, ask yourself, *Do my childhood memories deal with people, data, or things?* Your answer will provide a clue to who you are and what kind of work would be good to pursue. If your memories involve a lot of people and the emotions associated with those memories are enjoyment or excitement, then you should at least consider a position that puts your people skills to good use. If your memories involve the satisfaction of solving a puzzle by yourself, then you might consider a profession in which you're working with data or things, or a job in which you're not being drained every day by working with people. The private logic running through your childhood memories certainly doesn't limit what you can or can't do—people do change in radical ways—but recognize that your memories reveal your natural inclination. Listen to what your memories are telling you, then give yourself permission to explore what you're made to do.

Sometimes you just need that unedited reminder from your childhood memories to help you back on track to the life you were created for.

Business Sense for Your Birth Order

Jenny, the baby of her family, has an easy time making everyone who comes in contact with her feel like a million bucks. As a result, the clients she meets in sales meetings usually end up spending at least that much on her company's products. But while Jenny is the top salesperson in the region and can help clients immediately see the value of doing business with her company, when it comes to making major decisions regarding purchases or policy, unfortunately Jenny often makes them too hastily.

That's not an uncommon trait among lastborn children. Remember the birth orders we explored in chapter 4? Those patterns found in your childhood memories also apply in your work, and by paying attention to them you can not only learn your own strengths and weaknesses, you can also learn how to relate most effectively to those whose birth order differs from yours.

> If you are the baby of your family growing up, you probably have easygoing charm and a natural ability to get along with others, which is a great asset in management, sales, human resources, and any kind of up-front work.

Lastborns

If you are the baby of your family, you probably have easygoing charm and a natural ability to get along with others, which is a great asset in management, sales, human resources, and any kind of up-front work. We lastborns are likely to place a high value on social interaction and on integrating fun with work. On the flip side, however, you also might be tempted to make snap decisions from your gut rather than taking adequate time to weigh the pros and cons. You might even jump into volunteering for projects or serving on committees simply because you want to be where the action is. My caution to you lastborns, being one myself, is to consider waiting a bit before making major decisions—perhaps a couple days, if possible—which should shed light on your potential blind spot and keep your social strengths from becoming draining weaknesses.

> Middleborn children are usually good at seeing both sides of an issue—a strength in many kinds of business, politics, and law, among other areas.

Middleborns

Middleborn children are usually good at seeing both sides of an issue—a strength in many kinds of business, politics, and law, among other areas. All kinds of businesses need people who can be diplomatic and who can smooth the oceans of life in a storm. Middleborns are classic problem solvers, able to find bridges to solutions where others may not. Donald Trump, an entrepreneurial middleborn who also had a bit of the firstborn controller in him (having flip-flopped some birth-order traits with his older brother), said that it wasn't just making money that he enjoyed; it was putting together the deal—bringing two and two together.

You middleborns may have childhood memories of playing peacemaker in your family as you were growing up, which allows you to see both sides of an issue. But because of that you might also now defer decisions to someone else. Your propensity is to fade into the background and let others take charge—after all, that's what many of you did as children. In fact, a middleborn child might value compromise and making peace so much that she doesn't stand up for what she believes at work or in her relationships. However, your entrepreneurial skills may give you the push you need to overcome that weakness. Go for your idea, and it will probably fly!

Firstborn and only children are good at taking control of situations whether you're at home or at the office, so you might need to bear in mind that you're not always right.

Firstborn and only children

Firstborn and only children are good at taking control of situations whether you're at home or at the office, so you might need to bear in mind that you're not always right. You've had a whole childhood of exercising responsibility, sandwiched as you are between any younger siblings and your parents, so you've generally grown responsible in your work as well.

195

While we certainly need people to take charge, if you take too much charge you'll have people frustrated enough to charge you! Instead, focus your control in positive ways on the *situations* facing you, not on the *people* involved.

Remember that your strengths are not always strengths in every setting.

Your Greatest Strength = Your Greatest Weakness

Bill is an architectural engineer who can glance at a set of blueprints and immediately see whether "London Bridge is falling down." He receives big bucks as well as the praise of city planners and fellow architects for scrutinizing those drawings.

Is it any surprise that someone like Bill might have an early childhood memory of getting upset because someone messed up his little toy cars arranged in a line on his bedroom desk? Even as a boy, Bill saw a right way to do things—his way—and over time, his rigid, inner standards became benchmarks that he measured himself against. He's become extremely successful at work by following his way, and today he still has a few toys lined up neatly outside his house—not only his cars but also his jet skis and boat all in their proper places. Sadly, he not only pushes himself too far, but over the years he's come to use his inner rules as a standard for others, too.

In another of his childhood memories Bill remembers feeling an inner thrill and satisfaction at solving a puzzle (which his aunt had given him for his birthday) in only a few minutes and a touch of sadness that the anticipation was over. Bill's now "playing" with much bigger puzzles at work. Unfortunately, his private logic causes him to see everything as a puzzle to be solved or improved upon—including the chicken overcooked by his wife and their children's B+ grades among the As. By pointing out these flaws, Bill believes he's improving life for everyone around him, but will he be rewarded for finding flaws as he's rewarded at his job? On the job site, he might save hundreds of lives by spotting flaws. At home, his own life is in jeopardy by pointing them out!

The same skill that makes you a great engineer, accountant, or pastor can work against you in your marriage and family. Why? Because if you carry your ability to spot a flaw at one hundred paces into your relationships with your spouse and kids, you'll end up paying for doing it. Though Bill isn't into "this psychology stuff," he's precisely the kind of person who would come to see me because his wife was about to leave him. I would make the point with someone like Bill that the same skill that makes you a great engineer can work against you in your intimate relationships, which proves true in all the birth orders and lifestyles. And no one is more likely to run over others in his or her attempt to "make things better" than the firstborn son or daughter of the family or anyone who grew up with strict parents. That firstborn or only child, whose childhood memories typically include the theme of achievement, might feel that his rigid control makes the world a better place, even though it doesn't.

The lie Bill tells himself is that he only counts in life when he's in control, fixing the world's imperfections around him. Businesses fall head over heels for that kind of private logic when it comes to meeting sales quotas and generating profits, but apply those same standards to relationships at home and Bill's wife's "state of the union" address to him isn't going to contain very glowing remarks.

The same skill that makes you effective in your work can work against you in your intimate relationships.

Consequently, Bill's inner rules are causing his stomach to churn like a cement mixer, and he's developed all sorts of back problems and headaches. In fact, he's beginning to spend more time in the doctor's office than he does in his own office. If he had a mother who had hovered over him with worry as a child, saying such things as "Oh, be careful about getting too close to that! Don't touch!" then he already had a propensity to be a perfectionist that's only grown worse.

197

If you're a critical person—especially if you're the firstborn son or daughter or someone who grew up with a propensity to demand perfection from yourself because of your parents' expectations—don't "should" on yourself, as in "I really should do better" or "If I would have been on top of things, that should not have happened." Do that and you set unrealistic expectations that you could meet only in your wildest dreams . . . dreams that will become never-ending nightmares until you break the cycle of your sky-high expectations.

Bill needs to learn that his meticulous attention to detail belongs in the office, not the home, and that relationships aren't built in the same way as bridges. Instead, relationships must be seasoned with graceful love, especially in the times of failure, to keep from collapsing. If Bill is wise, the next time dinner is served, he'll be sure to leave his rigid rules for building structural bridges at the office and instead enjoy building relational ones.

Birth Order Strengths and Weaknesses

	POTENTIAL WEAKNESS IN RELATIONSHIPS	STRENGTH AT WORK
Firstborns and only children	Sometimes forget that they're not always right in relationships	Take control of situations at work
Middleborns	Tend to fade into the background because they're accustomed to compromise	Have great entrepreneurial skills and the ability to see both sides of issues
Lastborns	Can lose sight of maintaining discipline in relationships	Have an easygoing attitude that sets clients and coworkers at ease

Be a Shrink to Your Colleagues

Whether you volunteer on Sunday mornings helping your church's children's ministry or you're rushing around Wall Street's stock-trading floor, you brush arms and lives with people of all kinds. Wouldn't you like to gain insight into your colleagues at work to help you ride out the storm of office politics? Would you like to deepen your relationships and understanding of the mothers in your neighborhood play group (even if it's simply for your own sanity because several of them drive you crazy)?

If so, you might open a conversation with something like "Hey, I'm reading a book right now with an intriguing premise that's had me thinking about my childhood memories." That's a perfect chance to casually follow up by asking, "Can you recall any memories from when you were young?" Don't start by sitting down with someone over a business lunch and talking about private logic, lifestyle themes, and crucial reference points, because most people will say, "Whoa, I'm not so sure I buy that."

Instead, approach it from a storytelling angle. When you're standing around Monday morning talking about your weekend or sitting on the bench watching your kids play on the playground, ask, "When you think about your early childhood memories, what pops into your mind?" Most people aren't going to say, "Why are you asking that?" because it allows them to talk about their own life, and most people love the chance to talk about themselves.

If you talk frequently with someone you work with, applying the principles you've learned in previous chapters might give you clues to what makes them tick. As an aside, if you are in a management position and are interviewing potential employees, asking about their families as they grew up—or even their childhood memories, if it seems appropriate—is a great way to get inside the heads of potential employees.

Michael C. Feiner, a former senior vice president at Pepsico Europe, said this about birth order and his technique when interviewing potential employees:

> I usually ask one last question: "Can you tell me about your personal background—parents, siblings?" Then I just listen as tons of information begin to pour from the candidate. . . . This is the richest part of the interview in terms of learning about the candidate and the defining moments of his/her personal life. . . . Because getting things done in a large complex organization is so dependent on relationships, I probe quite extensively about family relationships and how the candidate carved out his/her own turf with his/her family.[1]

Even if you aren't a human-resources manager conducting an interview at your work, it helps to know your coworkers by casually exchanging stories from your childhoods. Not only will it give you great insight into why you relate to each other the way you do, it may help you avoid conflicts and streamline your productivity in your work environment as you learn how those around you see the world and their place in it.

Don't be shy. Give it a try!

People First

Professional financial investors will tell you that you should never buy stocks on emotion or impulse when financial news hits the stands. By then it's already history. Sadly, I'm sometimes drawn like a moth to the flame by the hype. To me, buying a skyrocketing stock is like walking in on one great big party—the more people, the merrier! Fortunately for you, you won't find my method featured in any upcoming issue of *Money* magazine. I'd probably have better odds of gaining on my investment at the county fair by hurling baseballs at milk bottles. So when I recently called my broker to sell a stock I owned, I found that in Leman financial-speak "the party was over" back when I had invested and that I had lost money.

As we continued talking, it quickly became apparent how very deliberate and professional my broker was in her speech. (Can you guess her birth order?) After a few more minutes, she made the comment that she was married.

"You're married!" I said. "I know of a book that you might be interested in," thinking of *Sheet Music,* my book on marital intimacy.

"Oh," she said, "I love to read!"

Her love of reading all but confirmed my suspicions about her birth order—firstborns love to read—so I took a stab and guessed out loud that she was probably the firstborn daughter in her family.

"Well . . . yeah," she replied. "How did you know that?"

"To go one step further," I said, "from the things you just told me about your family, I'll bet that your husband is the youngest child of his family."

"Yes," she said. "How did you know that?" I could just imagine her looking suspiciously over her shoulder, a bit taken aback that my guesses had been right on the mark. I mentioned my fascination with birth order and ended up suggesting that she read *Sheet Music* and *The Birth Order Book*. She said she would and after a few more minutes talking about our families we hung up, each having thoroughly enjoyed our talk.

I love interactions like those. When we began our call, I was nothing more than just another client. But within minutes, we were talking about our lives and had formed a relationship in spite of the fact that we were thousands of miles apart. I'd lost money on my financial investments, but I'd gained where it really counts: my relational investments. To me, that's "money in the bank."

There's so much more to business than making money. Whatever your childhood memories—whether they are filled with people or not—doesn't it make sense to put people first? Isn't that what makes life rich? Do you care more about your bottom line or about the lines you draw to nurture your relationships? Which matters more to you, making an extra two cents or taking time to share your two cents with someone?

Perhaps you've been working in the wrong job or utilizing the wrong skills and you're a fish out of water. Or perhaps you're in the right work, but simply need to rely more on the strengths you do have, not the ones others expect you to exercise. Wherever you are, whatever your family background and family makeup today, whatever you're doing in life now, your childhood memories can help you find your place in the world and pinpoint your strengths to move forward.

> Your childhood memories can help you find your place in the world and pinpoint your strengths to move forward.

I realize that for some of you, this journey of exploring childhood memories has been a painful

201

one. As a child, you saw and heard things that no one should ever experience in life. Reading through this book may have been a tough road for you, and I couldn't be more proud of you for the effort you've made—you're heading in the right direction! I hope the lessons you've learned will help you continue to navigate through life as you embrace understanding, grace, and forgiveness in the relationships that have wounded you so you no longer are subject to your past.

Those of you who have had an easier time in life may have also unearthed some priceless nuggets about yourself. Hold on to those! What are you going to do with those valuable lessons you've learned about your strengths and weaknesses?

Whether your journey through your childhood memories has been easy or difficult, I hope it's been a positive one. Do you feel you know yourself better having looked back at what you remember from childhood? Are you more aware of your private logic as you now move through your daily routine? Do you understand your lifestyle themes and are you able to catch yourself when you begin feeding yourself lies about when you count in life? Are you capitalizing on your strengths and growing through your weaknesses in your relationships and work?

Whether or not your past has been difficult, the question before you now is, What lies on the road ahead of you? When you close this book, will you endeavor to open yourself day after day to the possibilities before you?

Just think. Before you even knew what you wanted to be when you grew up, something inside you already knew and captured in images, stories, and feelings the person you were becoming and would be for the rest of your life.

This key to a positive present and future has been there all along in your childhood memories, stored way back when you were a kid. But it's up to you now to put that key into the lock and turn it.

Will you?

Mama, My Own Truth Therapist

When I think back to my childhood, it's a wonder that my family didn't tie me up in a potato sack and ship me off to the circus! I was a certified jerk to my brother and sister and didn't fit in at school unless you consider that seat on the other side of the principal's desk. With all the trouble I got into as a child, you might think that I would also have been at odds with my mother. But I wasn't. The irony was that I could talk with her about anything. *Anything!* We had an uncommonly close bond and nurtured that relationship every opportunity we had.

About five years ago, while spending the summer in New York state as my family and I usually do, I picked up my sweet mom from her home. As we drove through the neighborhood where I grew up, we were reflecting on my shenanigans and pranks as a kid and the fact that somehow—miraculously—I had turned out all right.

"We really fooled some people back then, didn't we, Ma?" I joked.

She laughed at that because I believe there were many times when even she was fooled and wondered whether I'd ever get my act together. She used to joke that she showed up at my school more than I did, and at times that probably wasn't far from the truth.

"I've always hesitated to tell you this," she replied, "but when you were in high school I prayed to God to please send just one C on your report card as a sign that there was something there."

I finally did get that C and then some. Even though I was barely able to graduate from high school, I made it through college, then grad school, and finally received my doctorate. If you would have told me back in high school that one day people would be calling me "Dr. Leman," I would have laughed at you. I love a good joke.

But because we so easily believe the lies of our private logic as we're growing up, we often see *ourselves* as the joke. What we need are others to help us see ourselves as we truly are, and my mother was the person who played that role in my life. She was the one who did take me seriously, my truth therapist who made all the difference for me. In spite of all those red Fs scribbled across my tests, report cards, and early years of life, she never stopped believing in me. She saw my limitations—she probably even saw some of her own shortcomings in me and unhealthy family patterns passed down through the generations—yet she continued to believe in me rather than allowing me to believe the lies I told myself. Eventually, her belief in me began to rub off and I, too, began to believe there might be "something there," as my mom had prayed. She was the best truth therapist I could ever have had and that visit together, as we shared our love and care for each other, I will cherish for the rest of my life.

Four years after that talk, my mother passed away on her wedding anniversary, New Year's Eve. As you can imagine, burying my mother brought back a flood of memories. With a mother, a friend as special and as close to me as she was, how could I not have cherished memories?

I was reminded of her influence decades before. It was an early spring day when my book *Parenthood Without Hassles: Well Almost* was released in the late 1970s. I had come to Buffalo, New York, as the guest of a talk show and was on my way back to catch a plane home to Tucson. As I drove toward the airport, however, something inside me, some homing instinct, pulled me toward my childhood home. I turned off the highway to drive through our old neighborhood, which was about a half mile from the bridge over Ellicott Creek.

It's a beautiful spot. I remembered how I'd spent nearly every day from late spring through the end of summer fishing for bullhead and watching the lazy days float by. In fact, I spent so much time around that creek that my buddy Moonhead's nickname for me was King of the Creek.

As I drove, I was so lost in thought that as I looked down from the bridge over Ellicott Creek I could have sworn I had slipped through a fissure in time and been swept back three decades. For there below me, on those same rocks where I used to fish, in the very same spot, was a little boy fishing. It was as if I were staring at myself. And there, sitting in precisely the same place where my mother used to sit with me, was a woman reading as she watched her son.

My head swam with the memories and my heart pounded faster as I pulled off the road, turned around, and doubled back over the bridge. Memories were coming fast, swirling vividly around me. I remembered myself standing there with my little fishing pole when I was only five years old and recalled how every summer my friend Moonhead and I tried to build a raft to sail to Tahiti—and how every summer the raft ultimately sank and we ended up drinking a little bit of Ellicott Creek. I remembered early morning trips down to the creek, like the one when I left my mother a note at 4:00 a.m. that read

> Mom,
> Went to check my traps. Don't worry, I've got a warm jacket on and gloves.
> Love,
> Kevin

You know by now how this works, so what do those memories tell you?

I believe they reveal that I was an adventurous little tyke, that I loved God's good creation, and that that little rocky shoreline along Ellicott Creek was very special to me as I was growing up. But I think those warm memories reveal an even more important point about my life—the central role that my mother played in nurturing me.

Though I grew up in the *Leave It to Beaver* era, my mother certainly wasn't a stay-at-home June Cleaver. She worked the graveyard shift as a nurse and as the superintendent of a convalescent home for children, after which she returned home to see us kids off to school. I remember once, when I was a kid, seeing my mother trudging down the street toward home through two feet of snow that had fallen the night before when she was at work. Winters can be treacherous in Buffalo, and the snowplows hadn't even cleared all the streets; yet there she was, struggling home through deep snow so she could care for us kids.

Care for us she did with the heart of a mama bear. She knew how much I loved fishing and often went out of her way to pack a lunch for the two of us—peanut-butter-and-jelly sandwiches, potato chips, and Pepsi colas—before we'd walk the half mile together to the creek. Then she would sit above me on a ledge and watch me fish.

Just like the other woman was doing with her little boy that spring day when I returned decades later. As I sat there in the car overlooking Ellicott Creek that sunny day, I felt compelled to do something for that mother who had unknowingly reminded me of my childhood and of how much my own mother meant to me. I was on book tour at the time, so I pulled a copy of *Parenthood Without Hassles: Well Almost* from the box in the trunk and inscribed on the inside:

> *Continue to take good care of that little fisherman.*
> *You're giving him memories he will remember for the rest of his life.*

I walked down to the rocky ledge, and when the woman turned around I simply said, "Here, I'd like you to have this." She looked up curiously, took the book, and thanked me. I turned and walked back to the car, started it up again, and headed toward the airport and home.

I believe God uses people in mysterious ways, putting them in your life for a reason. He certainly put that woman in my life to remind me how much my mother had given me. Perhaps he's used something in this book to remind you of those who have given to you.

There's a reason why we've looked so intently at your childhood memories. But as helpful as it is to walk through your past, how are you going to use what you've learned as you unlock and open doors into your future? Because that was then, and this is now. The life you live today is the past you'll soon remember. When was the last time you said to those who matter most in your life, "Thank you for believing in me"? I said those words to my mother on many occasions and, if I had the chance, I'd tell her a hundred times over again if she were alive today.

Like my mother who believed in me when there was little in my outward behavior to believe in, and like that mother sitting on the rocky ledge with her son while he fished, you're adding your own indelible imprints to the memories of those around you. One day—a month from now or decades from now as you're saying good-bye to someone you love—you may both look back on this very day. What will your loved one remember? What will you remember?

Never forget that, because the memory you're creating today may very well be one that will last for a lifetime.

Introduction: Think Back . . . Way Back
1. "Martin Luther King, Jr. Historic Resource Study," http://www.nps.gov/archive/malu/hrs/HRS1.HTM.
2. Cal Fussman, "Donald Trump, 57: What I've Learned: The Titan," *Esquire*, January 2004.
3. Anne Sebba, *Mother Teresa: Beyond the Image* (New York: Doubleday, 1997), 13–16.
4. "Young Bill Gates: $5 Bill," http://anecdotage.com/index.php?aid=139.
5. Marshall Frady, *Billy Graham: A Parable of American Righteousness* (Boston: Little Brown, 1979), 40.

Chapter 1: I Made a Fool of Myself . . . and Liked It!
1. Bronwyn Ritchie, "Overcome the Fear of Public Speaking with Mental Preparation Strategies." http://www.ezinearticles.com/?Overcome-the-Fear-of-Public-Speaking-with-Mental-Preparation-Strategies&id=185194.
2. See Romans 8:28.
3. David Willey, "Face-to-Face with Michelangelo's Genius," *BBC News*, May 25, 2004, http://news.bbc.co.uk/2/hi/entertainment/3744835.stm.

Chapter 2: The Little Boy or Girl You Once Were, You Still Are
1. Brainy Quote, http://www.brainyquote.com/quotes/authors/b/bill_cosby.html.
2. Michael Jackson, *Moonwalk* (New York: Doubleday, 1988), 11.
3. Ibid., 6.
4. Ibid., 9.
5. "Dispute Shuts down Jackson Ranch," *BBC News*, March 10, 2006, http://news.bbc.co.uk/1/hi/entertainment/4792028.stm.
6. "Michael Jackson Opens Neverland Ranch," *RTE Guide*, August 27, 2003, http://www.rte.ie/arts/2003/0827/jacksonm.html.

Chapter 3: Your Built-In "Aha!" Camera
1. National Cancer Institute, *Smoking and Tobacco Control Monograph No. 5*, http://cancercontrol.cancer.gov/tcrb/monographs/5/m5_foreword.pdf.
2. Beth Livermore, "Build a Better Brain," *Psychology Today*, http://www.psychologytoday.com/articles/pto-19920901-000024.html.
3. Carlin Flora, "Turning Moments into Memories," *Psychology Today*, http://www.psychologytoday.com/articles/pto-20031118-000001.html.
4. h2g2, "Bill Murray—Actor," http://www.bbc.co.uk/dna/h2g2/A7951412.
5. Bill Murray with George Peper, *Cinderella Story: My Life in Golf* (New York: Doubleday, 1999), 20.

6. Ibid., 18–19.

7. Neil Smith, "Denzel Washington Interview," http://www.virgin.net/movies/interviews/denzelwashington2.html.

8. Academy of Achievement, "Larry King," http://www.achievement.org/autodoc/page/kin0int-2.

9. Academy of Achievement, "Larry King," http://www.achievement.org/autodoc/page/kin0int-1.

Chapter 4: The Apple Doesn't Fall Far from the Family Tree

1. Family Communications, "Fred Rogers: Biography," http://www.fci.org/viewcontent.asp?sectionID=2&subsectionID={E83DD3B7-4304-4347-894F-20E9733DC19F}.

2. Family Communications, "Melodies in the Keys of Childhood: The Music of Fred Rogers," http://www.fci.org/viewcontent.asp?sectionID=1&subsectionID={824F0D6D-B199-4FF2-8475-2A897848D42B}&subsubsectionID={5CC812F1-E793-4569-B24E-D391F5733EE4}.

3. "Young Kiefer Sutherland: Out Cold," http://anecdotage.com/index.php?aid=20959.

4. IMDB, "Biography for Kiefer Sutherland," http://www.imdb.com/name/nm0000662/bio.

5. Roger Ebert, "The Movie Maker: Steven Spielberg," http://www.unlv.edu/programs/filmarchive/catalog_archive100/1968_amblin2.html.

6. IMDB, "Biography for Jay Leno," http://www.imdb.com/name/nm0005143/bio.

7. http://www.eagletribune.com/news/stories/20021012/FP_002.htm (This site is no longer available.)

8. Jay Leno with Bill Zehme, *Leading with My Chin* (New York: HarperCollins Publishers, 1996), 19–20.

9. Cal Fussman, "Donald Trump, 57: What I've Learned: The Titan," *Esquire,* January 2004.

10. "Donald Trump: Music Teacher," http://anecdotage.com/index.php?aid=13570.

11. The shillelagh is an Irish walking cane.

12. Edward Kennedy, "Navigating the Country Back on the Right Course," *Today,* April 20, 2006, http://www.msnbc.msn.com/id/12404515/.

Chapter 5: Your Lifestyle Has Nothing to Do with the Car You Drive

1. Found online at http://anecdotage.com/index.php?aid=7342.

2. "Interview with Tiger Woods," January 25, 2006, http://www.pga.com/ news/tours/pga-tour/woodsinterview012506.cfm.

3. Joe Robinson, "How We Live: Bring Back the 40-Hour Workweek— And Let Us Take a Long Vacation," *Los Angeles Times,* January 1, 2006.

4. Kathryn Spink, *Mother Teresa: A Complete Authorized Biography* (New York: HarperCollins, 1997), 3.

5. Anne Sebba, *Mother Teresa: Beyond the Image* (New York: Doubleday, 1997),16.

Chapter 6: Be Your Own Shrink

1. Anna Seba, *Mother Teresa: Beyond the Image.*, 13–14.

2. John Richardson, *A Life of Picasso. Volume 1: 1881–1906* (New York: Random House, 1991), 29. Information cited from Helene Parmelin, *Picasso Says.* Christine Trollope, trans. (London: Allen and Unwin, 1969), 73. Originally published as *Picasso dit...* (Paris: Gonthier, 1966).

3. Ibid.

4. Annie Murphy Paul, "This Is the Time to Remember," *Psychology Today,* March/April 1998, http://www.psychologytoday.com/articles/pto-19980301-000016.html.

5. Frank Sanello, *Spielberg: The Man, the Movies, the Mythology* (Dallas: Taylor Publishing Company, 1996), 2.

6. Robert Waldron, *Oprah!* (New York: St. Martin's, 1987), 34.

7. Ibid, 36.

8. Nicole Mowbray, "Oprah's Path to Power," *The Observer,* March 2, 2003, http://observer.guardian.co.uk/international/story/0,,905771,00.html and "Oprah Opens Up about Drugs and Abuse," *MSNBC,* http://www.msnbc. msn.com/id/9996876/page/2/.

Chapter 7: The Truth about the Lies You Tell Yourself

1. David Breskin, "Bono: U2's Passionate Voice," *Rolling Stone,* October 8, 1987, 44.

2. Found online at http://www.thecatholicspirit.com/archives. php?article=5550. (This site is no longer available.)

3. "Charles Monroe Schulz: Good Grief II," http://www.anecdotage.com/ index.php?aid=5995.

4. "Charles Monroe Schulz: Good Grief," http://www.anecdotage.com/ index.php?aid=1412.

5. Maryanne Garry and Devon Polaschek, "Reinventing Yourself,"

Psychology Today, November/December 1999, http://www.
psychologytoday.com/articles/pto-19991101-000039.html.
6. Daniel Schacter, "The Seven Sins of Memory," *Psychology Today,* May/
June 2001, http://www.psychologytoday.com/articles/pto-20010501-
000028.html.

Chapter 8: Avoiding the Wasted Years
1. Ephesians 4:26.

Chapter 9: Escaping the Parent Trap
1. "Jane Elliott's Blue Eyes Brown Eyes Exercise," http://janeelliott.com/
index.htm.
2. "Memory Quotes," http://en.thinkexist.com/quotations/memory.
3. Sharon Waxman, "The Scoundrel King," *Washington Post,* October 6,
1996, http://www.washingtonpost.com/wp-srv/style/longterm/review96/
fhackman.htm.
4. John Culhane, "Gene Hackman's Winning Wave," *Reader's Digest,*
September 1993, 88–89.
5. Ellen Hawkes, "The Day His Father Drove Away," *Parade,* February 26,
1989, 10–12.
6. "Larry King Goes One-on-One with Gene Hackman," transcript
of *Larry King Live,* July 7, 2004, http://transcripts.cnn.com/
TRANSCRIPTS/0407/07/lkl.01.html.

Chapter 10: The Inside Skinny on Those You Love
1. Hara Estroff Marano, "Secrets of Married Men," *Psychology Today,*
July 26, 2004, http://www.psychologytoday.com/articles/pto-20040726-
000013.html.
2. See Genesis 2:18.

**Chapter 11: Zap 'em with a Psychological X-ray (Your Kids Will
Probably Even Enjoy It!)**
1. "Growing Up with a Famous Father: Sometimes, Celebrity Dads Also
Know Best," *Ebony,* June 1996, 122–124.

Chapter 12: Are You a Fish out of Water?
1. Dr. Kevin Leman, *Winning the Rat Race without Becoming a Rat*
(Nashville: Thomas Nelson Publishers, 1996), 118.

Practical Wisdom with a Belly Laugh

An internationally known psychologist, radio and television personality, and speaker, Dr. Kevin Leman has taught and entertained audiences worldwide with his wit and commonsense psychology.

The best-selling and award-winning author has made house calls for hundreds of radio and television programs, including *The View* with Barbara Walters, *Today, Oprah,* CBS's *The Early Show, Live with Regis Philbin,* CNN's *American Morning,* and *LIFE Today* with James Robison. Dr. Leman has served as a contributing family psychologist to *Good Morning America.*

Dr. Leman is the founder and president of Couples of Promise, an organization designed and committed to helping couples remain happily married, and a charter faculty member of iQuestions.com.

Dr. Leman's professional affiliations include the American Psychological Association, American Federation of Television and Radio Artists, National Register of Health Services Providers in Psychology, and the North American Society of Adlerian Psychology.

In 1993, he was the recipient of the Distinguished Alumnus Award of North Park University in Chicago. In 2003, he also received the highest award that a university can extend to their own: the Alumni Achievement Award at the University of Arizona.

Dr. Leman attended North Park University. He received his bachelor's degree in psychology from the University of Arizona, where he later earned his master's and doctorate degrees. Originally from Williamsville, New York, he and his wife, Sande, live in Tucson. They have five children.

For information regarding speaking availability, business consultations, or seminars, please contact:

Dr. Kevin Leman
P.O. Box 35370
Tucson, Arizona 85740
Phone: 1-520-797-3830
Fax: 1-520-797-3809
www.lemanbooksandvideos.com

Resources by Dr. Kevin Leman

Books for Adults

The Birth Order Book

Sheet Music: Uncovering the Secrets of Sexual Intimacy in Marriage

Making Children Mind without Losing Yours

Sex Begins in the Kitchen: Creating Intimacy to Make Your Marriage Sizzle

7 Things He'll Never Tell You . . . But You Need to Know

What Your Childhood Memories Say about You . . . And What You Can Do about It

Running the Rapids: Guiding Teenagers through the Turbulent Waters of Adolescence

What a Difference a Daddy Makes

The Way of the Shepherd (*written with William Pentak*)

Home Court Advantage

Becoming the Parent God Wants You to Be

Becoming a Couple of Promise

A Chicken's Guide to Talking Turkey with Your Kids about Sex (*written with Kathy Flores Bell*)

First-Time Mom: Getting Off on the Right Foot (from Birth to First Grade)

Keeping Your Family Strong in a World Gone Wrong

Step-parenting 101

The Perfect Match

Be Your Own Shrink: 4 Ways to a Better You

Say Good-bye to Stress

Single Parenting That Works: Six Keys to Raising Happy, Healthy Children in a Single-Parent Home

RESOURCES BY DR. KEVIN LEMAN

When Your Best Isn't Good Enough

Pleasers: Why Women Don't Have to Make Everyone Happy
to Be Happy

Books for Children, with Kevin Leman II

My Firstborn, There's No One Like You

My Middle Child, There's No One Like You

My Youngest, There's No One Like You

My Only Child, There's No One Like You

My Adopted Child, There's No One Like You

My Grandchild, There's No One Like You

DVD/Video Series

Making Children Mind without Losing Yours (Christian—
parenting edition)

Making Children Mind without Losing Yours (Mainstream—public-
school teacher edition)

Value-Packed Parenting: Raising Rock-Solid Kids in a Pleasure-
Driven World

Making the Most of Marriage

Running the Rapids: Guiding Teenagers through the Turbulent Waters
of Adolescence

Single Parenting That Works: Six Keys to Raising Happy, Healthy
Children in a Single-Parent Home

Bringing Peace and Harmony to the Blended Family

Got a Question?
Log on to iQuestions.com

Available at 1-800-770-3830 or www.lemanbooksandvideos.com